STORE WINDOWS THAT SELL®

NUMBER 5

STORE WINDOWS THAT SELL®

NUMBER 5

Edited by Martin M. Pegler, SVM

RETAIL REPORTING CORPORATION • NEW YORK

HF
5845
S86
v. 5

Retail Reporting Corporation, 101 Fifth Avenue
New York, NY 10003

Distributed to the trade in the United States and Canada:
Van Nostrand Reinhold
115 Fifth Avenue
New York, NY 10003

Distributed outside of the United States and Canada:
Hearst Books International
105 Madison Avenue
New York, NY 10016

Library of Congress Cataloging in Publication Data:
Main Entry under the title: Store Windows That Sell® / 5

Printed in Hong Kong
ISBN 0-934590-39-7

Designed by Bernard Schleifer

Contents

Introduction

"All the world is a stage" — and the stage is filled with props; with gimmicks and decorative elements that enhance the setting — and can be used to create exciting displays. A "prop" is more than a mere supporting player; it sets the scene, — it is part of the ambiance, and creates the illusion which turns the featured product into a star attraction. It is all Theater, and Display and Visual Presentation are the Theater of Retailing. The displayperson needs only to look around him or herself to behold the wealth of "materials" available often for the asking or the taking. This is "stuff as dreams are made of" — and displays are dreams come to "life." The props define and distinguish as well as decorate these dreams.

It is impossible in a book of this size to incorporate and visually demonstrate all the prop ideas that exist around us. In Book 4 of Store Windows That Sell® we traveled in and out of local stores looking for "ideas"; in this volume we turn to the dictionary. As we flip the pages of this imaginary dictionary we stop to peruse a fraction of the possibilities that exist, but we do make mention, in the copy, of some ideas that though not illustrated will stir the displayperson's imagination. Thus, in pictures and words we hope that this Dictionary of Prop ideas will provide breakthroughs — will provide starting points — points of departure — glimmerings that will burst into full scale presentations. The displayperson will take the essence of an idea — shape it, form it, define it and personalize it so that the end result is something new and different — and especially suited to the particular product — the store's fashion image — and the target customer.

This is a source book. It gives answers to other people's problems. It shows how talented displaypersons and visual presenters found the ways and means to promote their products for their customers in their stores. They have taken cliches — ordinary everyday objects — and turned them into story-tellers — into legend makers — into effective selling displays. An apple is an apple is an apple — but when apples are racked up like billiard balls to promote menswear for fall — that is a personal and creative way of looking at and using common-every-day apples in a most uncommon way. Hopefully, that illustration will provide the talented displayperson with a ticket to a flight of fancy into an as yet unchartered way to make his or her apples attention getters.

Set the stage — light the lights — raise the curtain and let the SHOWING begin!

MARTIN M. PEGLER, S.V.M.

STORE WINDOWS THAT SELL

NUMBER

5

Chapter

1

A Antiques and things aged — Art, Artists and Art materials — Architecture and Architectural elements like Arches and Arcades — Apples with new applications — airships and airplanes — Animals like Alligators, Aardvarks, Antelope and all the assorted Antlered kind — Angels and Amorinos that go with Arrows and with or without bows and targets.

B Bamboo — Bark — Birch — Blooming Bushes — Birds, Bees and Butterflies — Birdcages for Birds or merchandise — Bags — Backgammon — Ball games like Baseball, Basketball, Billiards and Bowling — Baubles, Bangles, Beads and Bowls of Brass and Bottles of glass — Bricks to Build-up — Boomerangs to bring back — Blankets to cover floors or walls — Backstage settings at the Ballet — Books — Barometers — Bananas — Bikes — Blueprints and Butterfly nets.

C Cameras to catch the moment — Crates — Cartons — Cartoons, Caricatures — Cut-outs and Constructions — Croquet — Corrugated boxes, boards and papers — Clocks — Clotheslines and Clothespins — Clipboards and Chopsticks — Chairs — Chains — Chess — Checkers — Checkerboards and Checkered Cloths — Crystals and Chandeliers — Candles and Candlesticks — Chickens in and out of Coops — Cactus in Clay pots.

D Decks and Deck chairs — Dressforms to dress or to drape — Dropcloths — Dunes, Dune-fences and Dune grass — Doors, Doorways, and Doormats that say welcome — Desks and Desk chairs — Drafting tables and Drawing boards.

E Eggs for Easter and Egg-crates to keep them safe — Epees for fancy fencing — Easels to set up messages or merchandise — Eyes and Eye-glasses for getting things into focus — Egypt — Eagles — and anything Exotic.

Bergdorf Goodman, Fifth Ave., NYC
Angela Patterson, V.P. Store Planning & Design
Richard Currier, Dir. of Visual Presentation

Ralph Lauren, Madison Ave., NYC
Jeff Walker, Corp. Head of Creative Service

A is also for *alligators, antelopes* and *animals* of all kinds that are familiar and not too familiar. They don't have to come off the wall of a hunting lodge or out of a taxidermist's shop — though they could. They can just as easily and maybe even more effectively be fashioned anew out of papier mache — wood — whatever. The *animals* can be the sort one discovers in F.A.O. Schwarz stores; great big stuffed *animals* covered in plushy fabrics with wide smiling eyes and gentle, fangless smiles. Kids love them. Girls of all ages love them. Even all buttoned up business types soften at the sight of them.

A is also for *antlers* — for Christmas — for hat racks — for fun.

A is for *antiques* and anything *ancient* or *aged*. The recall the good old times — the bygone days that are always seen through a golden light. An *antique* can be old fashioned furniture — not necessarily pedigreed but quaint enough and unusual enough to appear charming — and interesting. *Antiques* do add interest to a presentation; they also provide a contrast. The display can point up what's very very new by showing fresh merchandise juxtaposed with something very very old — or seemingly old. *Antiques* aren't only in antique shops and museums. They are all around us — in barns — in attics — in forgotten corners — in second hand stores. The "ancient ones" can be found at auctions, bazaars and at house razings. Sometimes all it takes is some tender loving care to restore the piece to its almost original state and when all else fails there is paint and spackle — artwork and faux finishes.

Saks Fifth Ave., NYC
Michael Keith, SVM, V.P. of Visual Merchandising

Barneys NY, Seventh Ave., NYC
Simon Doonan, Creative Director

A is for *arches* and for *architecture* and *architectural settings*. The *arches* below are simple and easy to create and what makes them so effective is the rhythmic arrangement of the gracefully curved tops meeting and intersecting those in the opposing plane. The *arcade* (a run of *arches*) combines the soft feminine curve of the *arch* with the strong, elegant vertical line of the support and together send out a message that emphasizes the classic refinement and simple rightness of the merchandise being shown.

A is for *architrave* — the lintel or lowest of the three main divisions of the classic entablature and see, on page 10, what can be done when one takes the Porch of the Maidens from the Acropolis in Athens and turns it into a display setting that says "classic" and "elegance." Though the caryatid maidens support the entablature — if they were male figures they would be *atlantes*.

Evans, State St., Chicago, IL
Randal Axline, Visual Merchandising Director

Neiman Marcus, Wilshire Blvd., L.A., CA
Pala Persulas, Visual Merchandising Director

A is for *angels* and all sorts of heavenly, etherial and airborne things. *Angels* come in all sizes and shapes — from the amorini or little cherubs that are so necessary to the success of St. Valentine's Day — up to the life-sized Renaissance ones draped in damask, haloed in gold and almost kept earthbound by the size and weight of their feathered wings. Above: the wings are all that are needed to express the light, lovely and heavenly feeling of these white fur coats and jackets. The wings are constructed of paper-sculptured feathers on a buckram and wire frame and finished off with downy, feathery fluffs that soften the whole effect. Over to the far right — a graphic of a male angel saving a damsel in distress — unrelated to the subject on display though it does balance the composition.

A is for *apples* and *arrows* — and for hitting the target market with the message. The garments in Sonia Rykiel's display are *apple* red and the oversized *apple* on the floor says "red as an ——." The *arrows* serve as pointers — directing the viewer's eye and also adding some diagonal line excitement to the setup. On the opposite page we show a bright and different use for *all-American apples*. Here they are the symbol of *autumn* — a rich harvest — a glowing crop of appetizing beauties racked up and ready for the handsomely rigged forms to play with. Each form supports a cue stick and the triangular frames on the wall hold the *apples* in true billiard form. The empty rack is placed back on the wall to break the pattern — for interest — and the carefully arranged *apples* on the floor balance this beautifully staged and lit display. *Apples* say "pick of the crop" — "From A to Z" — "simple delicious" — and "ripe and ready."

Sonia Rykiel, Madison Ave., NYC
Design: Marc Manigault

Jordan Marsh, Washington St., Boston, MA
Linda Bramlage, V.P. of Visual Merchandising
Cindy Thrana, Boston V.M. Director

Alfred Dunhill, W. 50th St., NYC
Design: George Shimko

A is for *airplanes* in the *air* and the *airways*. It is for getting up and going places — flying off to remote or familiar places. It is *adventure* and it is excitement. All it takes is some model planes to set zooming through the windows or interior spaces to suggest travel — and they are as close and as available as your local model and hobby shops or better toy stores. Contact with an airline or a large travel agency may also land you a small *armada* of planes right in your windows. With the popularity of the bomber jackets and men's activewear, the *airplanes* make this a Top Gun

Lord & Taylor, Fifth Ave., NYC
Alan Petersen, SVM, V.P. of Store Design/V.M.
William Conrad, Fifth Ave., V.M. Director

B is for *birch* — *bark* — *branches* — *bamboo* with or without *buds* — *blossoms* and *birds*. These vertical elements know no season — always right — always adaptable. The *bamboo* poles and rods recall the Orient — the Tropics — romantic faraway places and settings for adventure. Whether used as long modular tubes to add excitement with diagonal lines dramatically cutting into a presentation, or bound and tied up with raffia or rope into semi-constructions or even cages — the *bamboo* helps to tell a story and set a scene. A raffia covered cat has been captured on safari and the bold adventuress now sits atop the cage holding the prized speciman on a fragile plained straw lead. With the fashion emphasis on animal prints and patterns — on South Seas colors and designs — the natural neutral *bamboo* is a dependable prop. It can be sprayed black for sleek, sophisticated dress-up displays or even gold when one dares to be different. The construction in the men's display not only serves as a foregound/background prop, it also holds some of the fashion accessories up at eye level. It could easily have supported rings of belts — stretched suspenders — rows of knotted ties — a spread of socks — and even a sweater could have been skewered through the bamboo before it was lashed.

Birch is usually silvery white and a harbinger of Spring or Summer. The tall, graceful, horizontally-marked branches suggest a forest — a place in the woods. For this Fall display the upright units are joined with moss-covered shelves and the mannequins are elevated off the wide ribbon-striped floor. The same turquoise and olive felt ribbons wrap the already nature-wrapped *branches* and they accentuate the colors of the merchandise being featured. Cool lights put a chill in the air and add another reason for the hooded stadium coats. The same bare *branches* of *birch* — without the ribbon band could become a seasonal holiday stand if the bark were hazed with diamond dust and the shelves were covered with red velvet.

D. Cenci, Madison Ave., NYC
Design: Perone/Allen

Bloomingdales, Lexington Ave., NYC
Joe Feczko, SVM, V.P. of Visual Merchandising
Robin Lauritano, N.Y.V.M. Manager

Lord & Taylor, Fifth Ave., NYC
Alan Petersen, SVM, V.P. of Store Design/V.M.

B is for *birds* and *birdcages* and what better place to put a *bird* in a *birdcage* than on an outside *balcony* with an ornate *balustrade*. To complete the illusion the designer opted for louvered doors over *blinds* and the vignette setting throws open the doors to a total Spring viewing. The merchandise is black and white — neutral — and even the setting is neutral. The back wall is painted sky blue and it is enhanced by blue filtered light. Up front lighting on the *birdcage* and the *balustrade* causes interesting shadows to appear on the background. *Birdcages* are a natural for Spring and they can be made of metal — be "antique" — gingerbread and curlicues — or they can be the inexpensive but very impressive kind made of bamboo and imported by the boatload. The *birdcages* don't have to house *birds*; they can shelter, support and show off shoes, small fashion accessories, cosmetics or jewelry. The cages can be elevated and bring the small, snared pieces up to viewer eye level.

D. Barneys, Seventh Ave., NYC
Simon Doonan, Creative Director

B is for *blueprints* and *blueprints* mean *building* and *build-ups*. They mean structures and structured. They refer to professionals — to craftspersons — designers and, of course, architects. "Constructed with Care" — "Built to Last" — "Blueprint for Success." This Barneys' window stresses the fine tailoring of the Armani suits and the *blueprints* are used to panel the backwall and the unraveling roll beneath the mannequins arm is leading the viewers eye to the Armani name stenciled on the front glass. *Blueprints* could promote blue, blue prints and patterns as well.

The *building* at Bloomingdales is really an open framework — a "birdcage" filled with home furnishings raised off the floor.

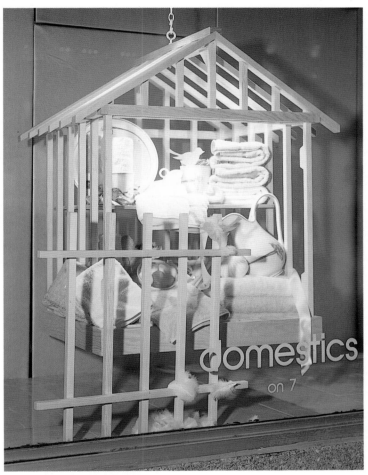

Bloomingdales, Lexington Ave., NYC
Joe Feczko, SVM, V.P. of Visual Merchandising
Robin Lauritano, N.Y.V.M. Manager

B is also for *beds* — *bedsteads* — *broomsticks* — and *bedrooms* and what could make a more effective setting for sleepwear or lingerie than a bedroom — or the essence of one. The bare bedstead frame becomes a playground for two of the mannequins while the third looks on ready with her pillow to join the "rumble."

Pages 22-23: Macy's, Herald Square, NYC
Steven Komajcik, V.P. of Visual Merchandising

Henri Bendel, W. 57th St., NYC
Danuta Ryder, Visuals Director

Macy's, Herald Square, NYC
Steven Kornajcik, V.P. of Visual Merchandising

B is for *blankets* — Navaho and otherwise. Whether for wrapping, covering or hanging on the wall — the Indian-style (and Mexican style) hangings make becoming South-western settings. The two displays above are filled with earthy colors and glowing warm lights and the *blankets, burlap, bleached bones* and *bowls* all add up to the readily popular look. Imagine what can be done with the Hudson's Bay Blankets for winter merchandising.

B is for *backgammon* — a game of chance that also takes no chances because the black/white and red color scheme is a winning one. Here the handbag is set into a shadow box backed up with bright red and the *backgammon board* is angled to support the tilted bag and the billowing shoulder strap. A *bull's eye* proscenium or mask frames the display. Right on target!

Boomerang begins with *B* and the *boomerang* brings back a message that is sent with a speedy sweep and a spin. This collection of freshly colored Thierry Mugler suits is accentuated by the swarm of spinning *boomerangs* in brilliant hues to match or contrast with the garments. The black setting and the strong light make the suits stand out — and the sunglasses are almost a necessity.

Henri Bendel, W. 57th St., NYC
Danuta Ryder, Visuals Director

Lord & Taylor, Fifth Ave., NYC
Alan Petersen, SVM, V.P. of Store Design/V.M.

B is for *brass — boxes — baubles — bangles* and *beads*. It is the bright, brilliant and burnished luster or sheen of the golden metal — and of the hand rubbed woods and the warmth they bring to an arrangement. This shadow box display overflows with small fashion accessories and is permeated by the scent and feel of the Orient or Near East. *Bowls* can hold smaller objects or be filled with atmospheric accents like spices, pine cones, candy or potpourri while *boxes* can be opened to reveal what is inside or be partially opened to allow the item to escape — to uncoil from its confinement and sneak in and out of the assembled pieces. *Boxes* of assorted sizes and shapes can also be used as elevations or risers to highlight clusters of coordinates or accessories.

Woodward & Lothrop, Washington, D.C.
Jack Dorner, Div. V.P. of Visual Merchandising
Jan Suit, Washington V.M. Director

Lord & Taylor, Fifth Ave., NYC
Alan Petersen, SVM, V.P. of Store Design/V.M.

B is for *buttons* and *brass buttons* especially since they speak of things nautical and military. When that "look" is in — or even if it is only for a Navy Blue promotion for Cruise or Spring — bring on the buttons. If fashion dictates that jackets will be buttoned and buttoned up with rows of shiny round buttons — play up the *buttons*. In this display overscaled replicas of familiar *brass* and horn *buttons* are applied onto the white back wall while the neutral carpeted floor gleams with the glint of myriad brass buttons; scattered at the mannequins' feet or lined up for a review. "Who's Got The Button?" — there is no doubt who has 'em and is showing them. If you can't get the bas relief kind — see what you can do with paper plates or assorted sizes — some gold spray — and clever touches of applique.

dresses.pure and si

on 3

Filene's, Washington St., Boston, MA
John Cunningham, Div. V.P. of Visual Merchandising
Russell Neubauer, Boston V.M. Director

Bricks — birds — bird's nests — and *baby's breath* all start with B. *Bricks* are for *building* — for creating structures and suggesting structure. *Bricks* are usually rough but even — coarsely textured — rugged, strong and basic and they can contrast with soft silky fabrics and gently styled fashions. In this presentation labeled "Pure and Simple" the bricks are simple and elementary — basic — and their rich terra cotta color adds warmth to the otherwise neutral setting and the "pure" black and white polka-dotted outfit. An Empire drape of bleached muslin provides a more elegant look and also contrasts with the *brick* construction up front. In the foreground — caught in a break in the brick-work is a *bird's nest* fancifully wrought of *baby's breath*. Safely nestled in the nest are some eggs. The whole scene is painted with warm, rose tinted light.

Macy's, Herald Square, NYC
Steven Kornajcik, V.P. of Visual Merchandising

B is for *barometer* — of brass or wood — nautical or not. *Barometer* can tell you when the wind is changing — where fashion trends are blowing — and where they are heading. They can be aged for more interest or antique for formal or classic presentations. This ship's device is setting the course right into cruise and Spring; taking the shopper where she wants to go especially if she likes navy and the nautical look. *Brass chains* are swagged across the upholstered back wall to simulate the railing on a ship and with the blue jacket, brass buttons and bullion stripes — it is full steam ahead into the new season. The swoops of brass chain could also work for a Chanel presentation when chains are in.

Marshall Fields, State St., Chicago, IL
Ken Smart, Div. V.P. of Visual Merchandising
Jamie Becker, V.M. Director, State St. Store

B is for *ball* — for all kinds of *balls* and *ball games*. It can stand for *basket ball* — with hoops and finished wood floors or brick walled school yards and concrete floors. *Billiards* begin with *B* and whether played with apples (see p. 17) or with the heroic sized *balls* that make such an impact in white, red and black in the Ungaro display — they score points. The *billiard sticks* give the mannequins something to hold on to and ties them, composition-wise, with the *balls* rolling around on the green felt covered floor boards.

B is also for *bowling* and this one will *bowl* them over. A realistic mannequin, dressed in a superb gown of black velvet finished with a swirl of cerise satin stands on a black and white checkered floor. She has made a perfect hit — even if one of the contrary pins refuses to lie down. The white pins emanate from around her like a starburst and the "culprit" — the *black ball* — joins in the set up. A hot pink filtered light floods the floor and washes over the mannequin. This is a *ball* gown in one!

Emanuel Ungaro, Madison Ave., NYC
Design: Marc Manigault

Before we leave the *B*'s let's consider the display possibilities of *ballet* — *ballet* settings — and theatrical *backgrounds* — bits and pieces of scenery — props — be-labeled trunks and such; always good for "Opening Night" — "Greet the New Season" — "Previews" — and most any theatrical expressions.

Books beging with *B* and *books* can go back to school — or college. They can fill in a library setting — fit in spaces on shelves crammed with school or career separates — serve as risers and elevations. *Books* say "smart" — "head of the class" — "the right or educated selection." In shadow box displays they can speak volumes and open up to choices. A mannequin carrying a book is a student — or a professional — but either way she is doing the right thing — in the right outfit.

B is for *bananas* and bright yellow promotions (see p. 71) — for *bikes* to set an active, sports theme or carry a mannequin in shorts through *Bermuda* — for *boxing* and *boxing gloves* and prize-winning decisions — for *butterflies* — *butterfly nets* and *bees* that can sting — and swell up a Spring window.

Marshall Fields, State St., Chicago, IL

Lord & Taylor, Fifth Ave., NYC
Alan Petersen, SVM, V.P. of Store Design/V.M.

C is for *checkers* — for *checker boards* — *checkered floors* — and *checkered cloths*. It is for hop-scotching blocks of color making strong patterns and big statements. For a Polkadot promotion the big red *checkers* are the dots and they are polka-dotted on the vignetted *checkerboard* that starts on the white wall and ends up on the floor of the window. Some of the checkers on the floor become elevations for the mannequins and others could be used up front to show-off perfumes and accessories. For sheer elegance and ballroom settings see what a *checkered* floor in black and white does on page 31.

Barneys, Seventh Ave., NYC
Simon Doonan, Creative Director

Any table covered with the familiar red/white *checkered cloth* becomes the spirit and setting for a bistro — a *cafe* — a smart sidewalk venue from which to watch the world go by. Add a loaf of bread (French or Italian) — a glass of wine — and a *candle* — and it is a romantic trysting place for young lovers. The place could be Paris — Venice — Soho or Poughkeepsie. Add plates of spaghetti and it is a Roman Holiday — as Italian as one can get and in our illustration the noted Italian fashion designer's picture is framed up behind the mannequin seated in the wire-worked chair.

The red/white *checkered cloth* is also fun — it is low key dining — the hash-house experience. The two handsomely dressed mannequins stand before a medium gray wall. Triangles of the squared off fabric are pulled taut against the wall and black and white artwork cups and saucers add the right touch to this flattened version of a dining room — or diner. Not as realistic as the other setting but it does get the message across and the red serves as a bright accent for the neutral clothes.

Alfred Dunhill, W. 50th St., NYC
George Shimko, Visuals Director

C is for *chopsticks* and who would imagine the *chopsticks* could be so much fun even when there is no food in sight and the product isn't even Chinese or Japanese? The repetitive bands created by lining up dozens and dozens of wrapped sticks make an interesting design across the back and floor of the window. Clusters of *chopsticks* are held together by sporty bow ties and they serve as risers for the humidors. This clever concept could be adapted to any other small fashion accessories and could also be "gilded" by mixing in some take-out *cartons* — the *carry-out containers* with the wire handles. The clean containers could hold some of the special treats and a pair of suspended hands — holding *chopsticks* could be drawing out a morsel; a necklace — a tie — a belt — a wallet — something small and that will fit in a container. You don't need a fortune *cookie* to know what the results will be.

C is for *clocks* and *clocks tell time and they are timely. It is "Time for ——" or "Time to ——" and when your forms or fixtures are headless — a clicking clock* can do double duty. In this display black *columns* support the suit forms and the background is splattered in black and white like the old fashioned writing notebooks. The dimensional swirls of yellow tie the three forms into an easy to read composition and note the red clock and the yellow pattern break what would be instead a static, symmetrical presentation.

Alfred Dunhill, W. 50th St., NYC
George Shimko, Visuals Director

Clips — *clipboards* and *cushions* that hold pins all begin with *C*. The rear wall is covered with a regular pattern of *clipboards* holding stats of suit construction — and the constructed suit is presented up front on a drawing table tilted to serve as a pin-up board. The red tomato *cushions* bespeak of "classic tailoring" and "made to order" fittings and they also add a color accent to the sedate window. Even the trousers are clipped on to board which is "held" by the classically rigged suit on the form.

Daffy's, Fifth Ave., NYC
Design: Mary Costantini

On the following pages *C* also stands for *crystal* — for *chandeliers* — for *classic* architectural drawings by artists like Piranesi — for *cornices* — swags and drapes — for *candles, candlesticks* — for a *clutter* of cosmetics, gifts, gift boxes and gift ribbons. Put them all together and what do you have? It is a sumptuous *Christmas* presentation that also includes the Phantom of the local Opera House lurking behind a *chandelier* — instead of the traditional Santa.

Pages 36-37: Macy's, Herald Square, NYC
Steven Komajcik, V.P. of Visual Merchandising

C is for *classic* — for *columns* — for *capitols* — for *cornices* — for *castings* of sculpture and *croquis* of designs. It also stands for *corbels* upon which shelves and *cornices* rest — for *cherubs* and *chairs*.

Macy's, Herald Square, NYC
Steven Kornajcik, V.P. of Visual Merchandising

Fendi, Fifth Ave., NYC
Mark Marcorbin, Display Director

Macy's takes a *classic* look at home furnishings with *columns* and *caps* — capped with pillows. *Casts* of familiar statues — stark white — people the setting and they are draped or toga-ed in bedsheets. A *corinthian cap* becomes a pedestal for paisley pillows.

Fendi gets as *classic* as *classic* can get with the gigantic casting of a muscular torso that fully fills the window and the actual merchandise, by comparison — or in *contrast* — is reduced to Lilliputian size.

The Bonwit Teller display features white outfits in an all-white ambience. The background is a relief *collage* of artifacts; frames, *casts, cones, cherubs,* ornate *corbels,* and bits of hammered metal. The chair is white-washed like all the other subjects in the display including the mannequins who are wearing barely blond wigs. The warm light helps to distinguish the elements by creating high lights and gentle shadows that shape the dimensional pieces.

Bonwit Teller, Trump Tower, NYC
Frank Calise, SVM, Div. V.P. Visual Merchandising
William Musso, Dir. of Window Presentation

Filene's, Washington St., Boston, MA
John Cunningham, Div. V.P. of Visual Merchandising

Marshall Fields, State St., Chicago, IL
Ken Smart, V.P. of Visual Merchandising
Jamie Becker, V.M. Director, State St. Store

C is for *cupboards* and *cabinets* and *curio cases* to fill with *china* and *crystal* — for *candlesticks* and *candelabra* — for *Chippendale chairs* (though these are after Sheraton) — and for *checkerboard* floors of black and white marble. It is for the *clutter* and *clustering* of *Christmas*. Filene's struck a musical note for their Holiday theme and "Gifts of Note" appeared on the front glass while the proscenium swag and drape was printed with notes and music bars. A harp, bedecked with garlands, ribbons and ornaments, filled in the room setting. In the center of the floor a collection of crystal, silver and decorative bibelots for gift giving and for *collectors*.

The *cupboard* used by Marshall Fields is a *country cupboard;* natural pine with provincial lines. Ground *cork* textures the floor under the old wood *crate* that serves as a platform for the display of coordinates and accessories. The coordinates are shown in a clean, polished, "rustic" setting and the visual merchandising is beautifully done. The display could be moved — as is — into the store and up front in a selling space.

A *chair* is a *chair* is a *chair* but it becomes something different and even sinister when shrouded in muslin and tied with twine. The Filene display of checkered and printed separates gains some dash and flash from the askew line-up of tilting *chairs* and the mannequin, on the floor, is basking in the glow of the golden light.

Gucci, Fifth Ave., NYC
Guy Scarangello, Corp. Director of Visual Presentation

C is for *cactus* in *clay* pots or growing out of boulders on a desert of ground *cork*. A cornice molding of natural pine serves as a shelf to cut across the blue and pink stained Southwest sky. On the shelf is a collection of assorted *cacti* growing in apricot colored *clay* pots and in some pots the plants have blossomed out with colorful reptile skin shoes boasting prickly tooth-pick spines. The effective lighting flushes the background with warmth.

The sun is setting over the *cacti* desert that has sprung up in the Jordan Marsh window. The background blends from gold to red and shadows are deep and vibrant. The outdoors setting is compatible with the neutral and desert-bleached colors worn by the semi-realistic white mannequins who need the dark glasses to offset the sun's rays.

Before the sun sets on this page let's mention some other *C*'s that grow in the Spring — in the Summer and Fall. *Calla* lilies are for brides and Easter — *crocouses* are for Spring — *Chrysanthymums* in yellow, gold and russet hues are Fall flowers — for "back to college" and "football games." *Corn* is golden and is harvested in the Autumn and *cornstalks* can make interesting backgrounds while the *corn* is cradled in baskets. *Carnations;* where would we be without red *carnations* for Father's Day and pink ones for Mother's Day.

Jordan Marsh, Washington St., Boston, MA
Linda Bramlage, Div. V.P. of Visual Merchandising

Lord & Taylor, Fifth Ave., NYC
Alan Petersen, SVM, V.P. of Store Design/V.M.

Bloomingdales, Lexington Ave., NYC
Joe Feczko, SVM, V.P. of Visual Merchandising

C is for *cats* that creep or leap and these *cut-out cats* strike a most contemporary chord for a Halloween setting. There is nothing scary — or hairy — about these two dimensional scored and folded creatures but they do create an ominous presence as they circle and surround the red haired mannequin. Imagine what can be done in a less sculptural way with black plush *cats*.

Cabanas begin with *C* and *cabanas* mean taking time out to *change* for swimming and sunning. The Bloomingdale *cabana* is made of striped cotton canvas and it is finished with a scalloped edge. Fendi's is constructed of foamcore and it is stylistically straight and sharp. Creamy sand is puddled on the light marble floor of Bloomies' window and these black-suited beauties are probably going to build sand *castles* but for the time being the middle one is playing black and white bongos. The backwall is flooded with lavender light and the mannequins are soaking up the yellow light of the incandescent spots. Fendi employs a bald headed form on a *clothespin* base and they are featuring red with black merchandise with their black and white cabana.

Clothespins and *clotheslines* are a fine way to hang up a variety of items and more can be arranged in the *clothes basket*. An electric fan, hidden, can cause a breeze to get the merchandise wafting in the wind.

Fendi, Fifth Ave., NYC
Mark Marcorbin, Display Director

Jordan Marsh, Boston, MA
Linda Bramlage, Div. V.P. of Visual Merchandising

America, Montreal, Canada

C is for *country* and in the *country* you find *chickens, chicken wire, chicken coops, chicken feed,* and — *chicken eggs.* In America the window is crammed with *chicken coops* containing *chickens* — feathers and all — and on the floor — a scattering of straw. The trendy twosome stand there amid flutter and fuss of *chicken wire coops* — completely aloof from what's going on — even the escaping rooster.

The *club* these Jordan Marsh kids belong to is definitely in the *city*. Here, *C* is for *chain link* fences, *cinder-blocks* and *cement* streets. It also stands for *cans* filled with litter — and skateboards for traveling. This urban setting is quickly recognized because with these few cliches the designers have created an enclosed school playground — or a building site where something is going up.

At Cindi's, they are just a bunch of *chickenheads*. The mannequins' heads are covered over with squatting chicken forms and to further the chicken experience — the girls are holding wire mesh egg carriers filled with brightly colored plastic eggs. Checkerboarded risers complete the setting.

Cindi's, Syosset, NY
Design: Mindy Greenberg, Bellerose, NY

Putumayo, Columbus Ave., NYC
Design: Jad Michaels

Reitman's, Place Bonaventure, Montreal, Canada

C is for *crates* — for *cartons* — for *cranes* — for *canvas slings* — and *clotheslines* with or without pins. The Putumayo sale consists of a stack of stenciled *cartons* wrapped up in a net sling being pulled up by a heavy cotton *cord*. The soft sculptured figure is doing all the work to get the message across.

The two world travelers have returned to Reitman's with their *crated* find — an ancient urn or a replica thereof. It has been carefully swaddled within the slat wood cage. Both mannequins are properly attired for persons on the go and the "discovery" or "artifact" adds a sense of the exotic and the mysterious to their going and coming. Note how both these display areas have *ceiling grids* — the heavy duty lattice work over the display area from which props or lights can be hung or attached.

When *comics* and *comic strips* are in — can *cartoons* be far behind? *C* is for *comic strip characters* — for *cartoons* and *caricatures* — for exaggerated drawings usually executed in *chiaroscuro* — dark/light — black/white. Palais Royal takes its cue from the gangbuster *comic* strip given a big Hollywood treatment and fills its window with *copy* in balloons floating over the "speaking" mannequins. Blasts of "BLAM" — "POW" and "ZAP" explode in the dark foreground. Illustrations identifying the two-dimensional hero appears in the arrangement.

Chiquenaude, Montreal, Cananda
Design: Yves Guilbeault, Montreal
Photo: Andre Doyon

Palais Royal, Houston, TX
John McCarthy, V.P. of Visual Merchandising

As a comic relief for showing and selling small fashion accessories, the designer for Ciquenaude has created *cut-outs* in a *crowd* to show off the store's wares. Black and white patterned ties, scarves, kerchiefs, belts and such are applied to the white board figures that are touched with black line details.

On the following two pages: Bergdorf Goodman goes all out with *cut-outs* — *cartoons* — and *caricatures* for a most attention-getting *carnival* of Fashions. Note how the mannequins are hiding behind cut-out cardboard masks and how the background captures the pulse and passion of New York City.

Pages 50-51: Bergdorf Goodman, Fifth Ave., NYC
Angela Patterson, V.P. of Store Design

Cameras Go Click at Palais Royal, Houston, TX
John McCarthy, V.P. of Visual Merchandising

Going Coconuts at Sonia Rykiel, Madison Ave., NYC
Marc Manigault, Design

Bonwit Teller, Trump Tower, NYC
Frank Calise, SVM, V.P. Store Design/V.M.

B. Altman, Fifth Ave., NYC
Arthur Crispino, V.P. of Visual Merchandising

D is for *dress form* and a *dress form* is more than a fixture — more than a replacement for a torso — more than a stand-in for a mannequin. A *dress form* is all that and also a prop, a decorative element and a status symbol. A *dress form* means custom tailoring — a designer's line — a touch of class and refinement. It just wouldn't be Ralph Lauren Polo without a *dress form* to wear the merchandise. A couturier couldn't do couture without a *dress form* to drape on — a canvas covered one complete with wire cage skirt and cast iron base. Don't ever think a *dressmaker dummy* is dumb. It is the epitome of smart! The form can be accessorized with an upholstered egg head that replaces the brass neck plate and articulated arms can be attached at the Venus de Milo shoulder line. The *dress form* can wear a stitched canvas — a pattern-in-progress — a wealth of accessories like scarves, belts, and bags loaded or tied on — or it can be finished in damask or velvet and be beautiful and shapely just as it is. For a Spring promotion it can even be veneered with moss and accessorized with sprays of ivy and garlands of flowers. Of course, you could always dress it.

Barneys, Seventh Ave., NYC
Simon Doonan, Creative Director

H.A.E. Smith, Hamilton, Bermuda
Wm. H. Collieson, V.M. Director

D is for *decks* and the *deck chairs* on them. The Saks window subtly suggests the sea going locale with a hand rail up against the front glass — a deck chair opened and ready to receive the Chanel-suited voyager — and another folded and leaning against the paneled wall just in case "someone" comes along and makes it a shipboard romance — or "An Affair to Remember." To be on the safe side, a life-saver is ready and waiting just in case the sidewalk voyeur didn't recognize the shipboard setting.

Ann Taylor, E. 57th St., NYC

D is for *driftwood* and *driftwood* is carved by nature and the elements into marvelous one-of-a-kind sculptures. To set off the expected formal symmetrical arrangement that seems to go with fine china and crystal, the designer has selected a barnacled and be-coraled piece of wood to serve as the centerpiece of this composition. A chunk of styrofoam has been carved by the artist (not nature) to resemble the dynamic driftwood that pierces it, and the base also serves as an elevation for some of the wares. Note how the silverware has been plunged into the base. Bits of coral and sea smoothed pebbles are scattered about on the floor of the display.

D is for *dunes* and also *dune grass* and *dune fencing* — all associated with the sandy hills that rush down to meet the turquoise sea. In this accessory shadow box the blue background complements the sand on the floor and all of Nantucket or Cape Cod comes into sight with that bit of wood and wire fencing and the sprays of hardy grass. These shoes were meant for striding by the seaside.

Saks Fifth Ave., NYC
Michael Keith, SVM, V.P. of Visual Merchandising

Alfred Dunhill, W. 50th St., NYC
George Shimko, Visuals Director

Macy's, Herald Square, NYC
Steven Kornajcik, V.P. of Visual Merchandising

B. Altman, Fifth Ave., NYC
Arthur Crispino, V.P. of Visual Merchandising

D is for *darts* and *darts* are a smart way to make a point. It hits the target — it scores and you can't help but be the winner especially when all those centers say there is a sale going on. Another smart thing about this display is the rigging of the form. The pants are pinned sideways, under the jacket, and they drape naturally down to the floor covering the wood base that supports the suits form. Also — as a casual touch, the Sinatra coat-slung-over-the-shoulder routine and in the other hand a *dart* ready for another throw.

D is for *desks* — for school *desks* for kids or career-minded persons or *drafting tables* or tiltable artist's desks for professionals. The designer at B. Altman has an ergonomic posture chair to go with her *desk* and on the floor is a portfolio with fashion sketches; one not unlike the outfit she is wearing.

For "back to school" the impish kids are acting up on traditional, old-fashioned school *desk* and seat combos that are probably more recognizable by the parents than by the children. A blackboard bands the backwall and teacher is well dressed but she seems to be having a hard time and the term hasn't really started yet.

Henri Bendel, W. 57th St., NYC
Danuta Ryder, Visuals Director

Miller's, Pittsburgh, PA
Design: David K. Hopper

E is for *eyes* and the *eyes* definitely have it. "In Fashion's Eye" — "Eyes On" — "All in Favor Say ——." This wildly exuberant display is a sure shopper stopper and it is basic — it is simple — clever and thoroughly thought out and carried out. On the front glass the artist has painted, in black, many "fashion" *eyes*. More *eyes* have been loosely sketched on the white rear wall. The floor is also covered with white and here too the artist has grafitti-ed, lidded and lashed *eyes*. All these *eyes* are on the two veiled figures in evening gowns. The viewer is "forced" to look where everybody else is looking — at the center of all that interest. The wigless mannequins stand off center in the open space with a pink light on them — and they are worth staring at.

E is for *eye glasses* — which go with *eyes* — and this promotion borrows the movie title to say — "For Your Eyes Only." The giant scaled black frames are cut out of foamcore and one pair is set high at the glass line — one is low, up front, and the third set is folded and just coming off the rear wall. They surround and scrutinize the contemporary forms which are used in place of mannequins. The eyeless, flat oval "faced" forms are completely accessorized for the showing.

E is for *easels* and *easels* mean art and artists. *Easels* hold signs as well as paintings and paintings mean form and color.

For the Mondrian-inspired outfits shown at Level One, the *easel* carries the message "Wearable Art" and blocks off the basic colors associated with Mondrian's art are introduced. Instead of a hat or wig the mannequin carries a headdress of rectangles and squares in colors coordinated with the outfit she's wearing. A simple folded foamcore screen, a la Mondrian, completes the "artistic" composition.

Below it is Jackson Pollack time and these *easels* support splattered, splotched, be-dribbled and be-dabbed canvases that echo the colors and designs of the "paint stained" separates worn by the artists. Here, too, the usual wig has given way to twists of ribbons and scarves and the palettes become fashion accessories. "Art Forms" is what it was called at Filenes.

E is for *eggs* and it is also for *egg crate* materials and the neutral gray paper-pulp shaped sheets are easily recognized and remembered by some of us. Here the bas relief panels are painted to blend with the colors of the separates and some are sculpted to surface a seat for the mannequin while others serve as background panels.

Level One, Condado Beach, San Juan, PR
Frank Caballero, Designer

Filene's, Boston, MA
John Cunningham, Div. V.P. of Visual Merchandising

On the following two pages we show *E* as in *epee* — or *F* as in *fencing* for those who don't do the Sunday crossword puzzle. Either way there is a lot of swashbuckling going on in these most untraditional holiday windows. The damsel in distress doesn't look distressed though her bouffant skirt — a framework of distressed 1 x 2 lumber certainly isn't looking too perky. Her pannier is made of mistletoe and the pompadour is composed of dried and tinted hydrangeas. The duelers are in full action — swinging from a grapevine chandelier and perched on an overturned chair. The clothes are by Azzedine Alaia.

We leave you a few *E*'s to ease our display ideas. *Egypt* is *exotic* — it is antiquity — it is mystery — the Sphinx, pyramids, papyrus columns and blossoms, King Tut and Queen Nefetiti. *Eagles* soar and personify the American way. *Easter* goes with *eggs* — and lilies and tulips and straw hats with ribbons. AND — *everybody* loves *elephants* who remember anything.

Palais Royal, Houston, TX
John McCarthy, V.P. of Visual Merchandising

Pages 64-64: Barneys, Seventh Ave., NYC
Simon Doonan, Creative Director

63

Azzedine Alaïa

F

Flags on and off Flagpoles — Frames to Frame or to Focus — Fish, Fishing, Fishing nets and poles — Fruit — Flowers for all seasons and holidays and Flower pots to hold them or to build up with — Fences of wood or wire or Fencing for Fun and sport — Flashlights to light up a white on white setting — Feathers to Float, to Fly or to tickle one's Fancy.

G

Gardens, Garden Gates, Garden furniture and Gravel for the Garden path — Garbage cans and Garbage can art — Globes — Glasses — Garment bags — Giraffes for things tall and Gingerbread figures for things small.

H

Hammocks of Hemp for Holiday leisure — Hay as in Haystacks and in bales of — Hares like bunnies and hoops to jump through — Houses, Homes and Home Furnishings to furnish display settings — Hangers for Hang-ups — Hats, Hat boxes, Hat racks and elegant old Hat Stands with Hooks for hold and show — Harps and Harpsichords to reach the Heart and the Hands to play them — Helmets for war or for sport — Horns for blow or show — Hydrants to set a city street.

IJ

Instruments for making music or for scientific blending or measuring — Inflatables that make big statements with hot air — Irons and Ironing boards — Imagination.

Jellybeans in big glass Jars — Jig-saw details on Victorian gingerbread houses — Jig-saw puzzles with pieces missing or to fit in — Jesters to make merry — Jacks to toss for colorful merchandise.

K

Kitchens and Kitchen appliances including the Kitchen sink — the Kitchen cupboard with Ketchup in squeeze bottles — Knots tied in ropes — Knights in gray armor — Kites with long tails to carry skyward messages of spring and summer.

Giusti, Plaza Americas, San Juan, PR
Frank Caballero, Designer

F is for *fences* and *frames* and in this display they combine to give *form* to an illusion of a cottage for a promotion for home fashion accessories. Window *frames* are flanked by louvered shutters and the fine china is integrated into the open squares of the glassless panes and on the window ledge which is actually the floor of the window. If Fiddler on the Roof can be a smash — why not Dishes on the Roof? A cedar shingled "roof" cuts across one end of the window to support an above eye level showing. It also backs up the floating frame. Behind the open window on the floor — pink geraniums for a country cottage feeling. It is the picket *fence* that really says "home" — the pattern and continuous rhythm on the pickets throughout the display composition.

Woodward & Lothrop, Washington, DC
Jack Dorner, Div. V.P. Dir. of Visual Presentation
Jan Suit, Washington V.M. Director

Marshall Fields, State St., Chicago, IL
Ken Smart, Div. V.P., Dir. of Visual Merchandising
Jamie Becker, V.M. Director, State St. store

F is also for *fenders — fender-benders —* and *fences* made of wire mesh instead of wooden pickets. The Cyclone *fence* screens the window and behind in the glow of hot pink light is a dismembered or severed car surrounded by gleaming chromed hub caps. Panels of vacuum formed plastic emulate a brick wall and that wall is decorated with trophies of the chase. This hot-rodders fantasy was a back-to-school promotion for trendy teenage students.

Macy's, Herald Square, NYC
Steven Kornajcik, Div. V.P. of Visual Merchandising

F is for *frames* and *frames* frame; they contain — they close in — focus in on — enhance and they also say "art." On page 66 the Giusti window tied in with a Gaugin theme and instead of showing the Gaugin paintings the display featured separates in prints that might have been originated by Gaugin in a commercial moment in Tahiti. The assorted gray/white *frames* — though unfilled — manage to turn the printed garments into "paintings." Note the use of the *frames* to create a "composition" of the accessories on the floor.

At Macy's old gilded *frames* create a classy setting for a Mother's Day lingerie promotion. The mannequin is shown off center and she is balanced and complemented by the massive period *frames* to her side and behind her.

F is for *fruit* — *fruity flavored* and *filled* hats and headdresses. *Fruit* goes with the tropics — with cruise and resort wear — with fun and frolicsome fashions. Carmen Miranda never had it so good in her tooti-fruitty hat as these swim suited ladies at Bendel's in their strawberry, cherry and lemon-lime outfits.

Henri Bendel, W. 57th St., NYC
Danuta Ryder, Visuals Director

Gimbels, NYC

Bananas are big on top at Gimbels when it comes to adding some pizzas to yellow, white and aqua separates. Yarn wrapped balls, on the floor, double as oversized *fruits* while the white turbans are enriched with clusters of bananas and whisps of raffia. Even the earrings are *fruitty* dangles.

F is definitely for *flowers* and *flower pots* — filled or unfilled. The Macy's display, on the following page, has a background of *framed* latticework and a swirl of grapevining that twists through the display unifying the pots with the hung merchandise and the floral sprays. The large *flower pots* on the floor are sprouting Spring/Easter outfits — a-bloom in color. The oversized pink roses add bright accents in this pink lit setting.

In Woodward & Lothrop's display the *flower pots* become building blocks and they are stacked, shelved, and even inverted to show off the accessories that bloom in the Spring; shoes, belts, and bags. An exquisite balance is achieved in this arrangement and the dried flowers and whispy Spanish moss supply a softening quality to counteract the crisp, clean construction of the pots and the shelves.

Macy's, Herald Square, NYC
Steven Kornajcik, Div. V.P. of Visual Merchandising

Woodward & Lothrop, Washington, DC
Jack Dorner, Div. V.P., Dir. of Visual Merchandising

Jordan Marsh, Washington St., Boston, MA
Linda Bramlage, Div., V.P. of Visual Merchandising

Flamingos are *flame* pink and they start with *F.* With or without *feathers* these long limbed S-shaped symbols are often associated with Florida — Miami Vice and the southern climes. They are Art Deco and even High Camp and they do work as high color accents in resort and cruise promotions. In this window the merchandise is neutral — almost gray, black and grayish yellow — as subtle and Oriental as the mannequins wearing the outfits. The shot of hot pink created by the plastic replicas on the green-grass carpet is a light, bright — and amusing touch.

F is for *flash* — and the *flashlights* that as cylinders of illumination light up the scene. The presentation is white on white — and in all that whiteness it does take expert lighting to form those small ovals of brilliant light in front of the white, white torches lying on the floor. The white *flashlights* and the white copy on the wall salute "Light Up Atlanta." Note how areas of the window are left in shadow so that where the light is focused it seems even brighter than it is because of the contrast.

Marshall Fields, State St., Chicago, IL
Ken Smart, Div. V.P. of Visual Merchandising
Jamie Becker, V.M. Director, State St.
Amy Meadows, Manager, State St. windows

F is for *fun* and for some *fishing* is great sport. With it goes all that *fishing gear* including *fishing rods* or *pole,* and *fish nets.* The sign across the window reads "Gone Fishing" but they've left their poles standing in a row across the window — like a crop of bamboo rods. The bobs are bobbin and the ladies are taking no chances on what the day will bring so they are bringing the catch of the day with them. *Fishing* suggests "nice and easy" — relaxing — time off — leisure and the *fishing* equipment is as close as the nearest local game and hunt shop — or sportswear department — unless you've got some gear tucked away in some dark closet just languishing away. The rods give the mannequins something to hold on to and the lithe poles can also be used to add vertical or diagonal lines to the composition — to point or direct the viewer around the display.

F is for *flowers* and *flower shows.* On the following pages is a typical extravaganza of *floral art* as featured in Macy's annual Spring Flower Show promotion. Sometimes the settings are enhanced with *fountains* and garden statuary but this one takes the viewers down south to Louisiana for a lush, informal garden with Spanish moss dangling overhead in the electric *fan* breeze. The *filigree* ironwork is an integral part of New Orleans *facades.* Behind the forward balcony are two floor-to-ceiling louvered doors leading into the "house." The expert lighting enhances the pink and red blossoms — keeps the green looking green and suggests a depth to the window that is pure illusion.

76

The laydown of menswear on the textured and weather
worn board is propped with a *fishing rod* and *net*. This is a
wonderful study in textures; the background, the board, the
sweater, the wire mesh basket and even the ribbed socks.

Pages 78-79: Macy's, Herald Square, NYC

I. Miller, Fifth Ave., NYC
Howard Nevelson, Visuals Director

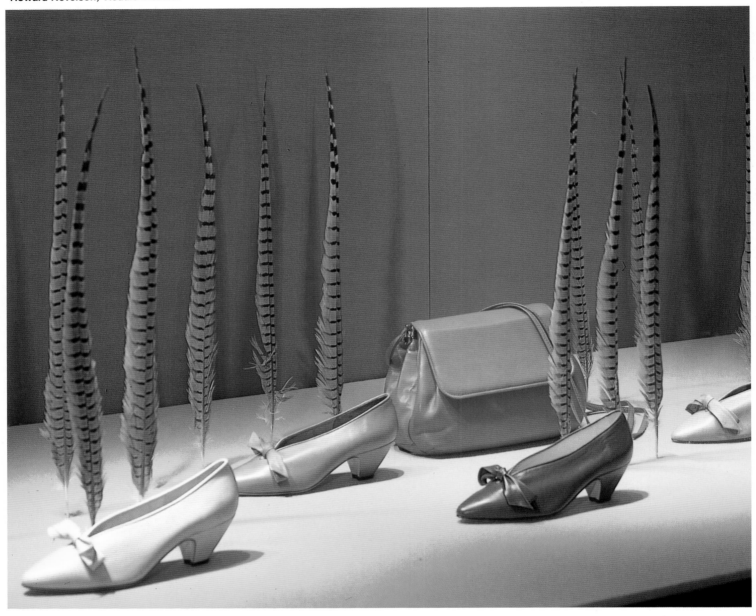

Feathers are light — bits of *fluff* that float and fly and fill the air with the feeling of flight — and the quality of fragility. In the accessory display the *feathers* stand upright — tips into the floorboard and say "light as a ——," "walking (floating) on air," and "feather light" since *feathers* do seem to float in the air and are so light. Since the shoes and bags are all following the horizontal line and the long, horizontal line infers a relaxed and easy going way, the guardian *feathers* become the vertical lines of the composition and bring to the display the idea of class and elegance usually implied in vertical lines.

The mannequins in the flowing white lingerie and nightwear are standing in a downpour of white *feathers*. On the floor; banks of *feathers* fill the space with down. Instead of the traditional wigs the mannequins are fitted with *feathered* cloches and draped over them are lace-trimmed, luxurious pillow cases.

G is for *gravel* — for *gardens* — for *garden furniture* and for the *gates* that enclose them or open up for vistas of viewing. The Gucci window is designed to look like the entrance to a country estate and the handsomely dressed equestrians are enjoying their weekend away. White *gravel* covers the "road" and the latticework, the posts and the architectural elements suggests the manor house beyond. The jockey rein-holder fits in with the "horsey" set while the overflowing ivy adds the right touch of garden greenness.

At Ann Taylor, the ivy entwined topiary trees become a verdant bower thanks to the white, Victorian-styled, cast-iron, *garden seat* which is the focal point of the composition. The mannequins are all wearing separates and sweaters enriched with brightly patterned trim. The floor is white and the window is open backed leaving a semi-view of the shop interior.

Henri Bendel, W. 57th St., NYC

Ann Taylor, E. 57th St., NYC

Gucci, Fifth Ave., NYC
Guy Scarangello, Corp. Director of Visual Presentation

Barneys, Seventh Ave., NYC
Simon Doonan, Creative Director

G is for *garbage cans* — *garbage can art* and *garment hangers*. The horse's body is a *galvanized* can and the cover has been bent into a head. Bits of scrap metal serve as ears and pipe cleaners and snips of plastic tubing become the mane and forelocks near the hooves. The "legs" are discarded T.V. carts on casters. The accompanying animal is another fantasy fabricated of metal remnants and *garbage gleanings*. The suit is rigged on a dressform and suspended off an antique *"gallows."*

Garment bags and *boxes* are for more than sending *garments* out of the store or for covering them in transit. They are the store's ambassadors-at-large who travel widely proclaiming the store and its merchandise. *Garment bags* and *boxes* can fill an up front area with the news of a sale and do it with humor — style and imagination. These cut-out forms with bendable arms and legs are all *gussied* up; dressed, draped and turbaned in store name imprinted plastic bags — and there isn't a single piece of merchandise on view nor need there be. The high-tech fixture with the oversized casters is usually used on the selling floor to hold the show stock but devoid of garments it becomes a contemporary structural design and elevates the rear cut-out into prominence.

G is also for *globes* and *globes* are for travel and back-to-school promotions — for *games* of chance where the shopper always comes up with the winning combination — for *gingerbread houses* and *gingerbread boys* and *girls* always ready for use in a Christmas trim — for *giraffes* for a neck up and *graduation caps* and *gowns* for career-oriented *gifts*.

Jess, Westside Pavillion, Los Angeles, CA

Barneys, Seventh Ave., NYC

H is for *hammocks* — for *hemp* — for *holidays* and easy sways, whether used as exotic scarves or mantillas or *headdresses* — or strung out between wooden dowels and hung from conveniently located neighborly palm trees. The *hammock* tells the viewer to relax — take it easy — stretch out in the sun or shade and enjoy. The woven strands of twine create handsome patterns and make fascinating shadows on the wall and floors of the display window. The swinging, swaying *hammock* in Barneys' window is festooned with tassels of the twine that are entwined with seashells and star shapes. The mannequins are dressed in sportswear separates in beige and brown which with the neutral color of the *hammock* exemplifies a neutral, monochromatic display. The cool blue light streaming in from the right meets the flush of the red from the left to make light lavender shadows on the rear wall — and to spike up the colorless presentation.

Bergdorf Goodman, Fifth Ave., NYC

H is for *hay* and *hay* is straw. *H* is for *hares* and *hares* are rabbits. So, *hare* in the *hay* or bunnies in the straw — it is *hoedown* time and a fun way to say country-style dressing. The window is crammed to overflowing with bales of straw and *hares* by the dozen are romping and stomping through the *hay* that reaches up to the rough-hewn wood shelves on the walls. An entire family seems to be hiding in the straw and they are more likely to find a *hare* than the proverbial needle in the *haystack*.

The nice, neat and tidy bales of *hay* in the shoe and boot display serve as effective elevations for the western-style merchandise without the other usual cliche props. Each level offers another group for viewing and the shopper's eye works up from the neutral, earth colored floor — by stages from below eye level to eye level to just above eye level. The louvered panels behind conveniently screen off the store's interior from the window area but the "down country" and "western" attitude comes from the stacked bales.

La Marca, E. 57th St., NYC
Toshi Studio, NY, Design

88

Complexe Desjardins, Montreal, Canada
Yves Guilbeault, Designer
Andre Doyon, Photographer

H is for *hoops* — *hoopla* — *hoop-de-doo* and *hip-hip-hooray!* These simple rings of wood, plastic or metal are also hip for *hula-hooping.*

At Minna's there is a dog act in progress and the attention-getters are "jumping through *hoops*" to play up the "ring-mistress's" scarlet suit with shiny brass buttons. The setting is all black; the *hoops* are bright yellow and the organdy ruffs around the performers' necks are red, yellow and black. The lady stands on a *hoop*-bound riser for prominence and though there isn't much action going on at the moment — any moment a *hound* will *hop* through a *hoop* and it will all be worthwhile.

Minna, Itokin Plaza, Madison Ave., NYC
Sylvia Graham, Visuals Manager

Circus Maxima fills the Bendel main window and it's enough to bring out the beast in anyone especially if they are dressed for the occasion. The cat masked mannequins are wearing assorted animal prints and patterns and they are trained to go through their performance paces; leaping through *hoops* — perching on pedestals — balancing on balls. All the props are black and white, the mannequins are black and the tawny animal prints are bathed in deep red and blue light that fills the center arena with drama — and anticipation. *Hooray* for the animal acts.

Henri Bendel, W. 57th St., NYC
Danuta Ryder, Visuals Director

Household and *home furnishings* get a very special setting with these geometric forms; hollowed out openings in cubes — right angle shapes of smooth plaster and a single classic column to support the sleek forms. Sheets, pillowcases, quilts and matching accessories are spread about, stacked, draped and drawn through the white forms in this white on white setting. As in many of our selections it is the expert lighting of both foreground (merchandise) and background that make this such an effective, dimensional display.

Aggio, Newport Centre, Jersey City, NJ

94

H is for *hangers* — *hangars* (for airplanes and take-offs) — for *hang-ups* (like in pin-ups) for *hats* and *hat racks*. "Mommy Dearest" made the wire kind notorious but at Aggio the plastic ones which are available in myriad colors become a suspension bridge swinging from semi-realistic mannequin to mannequin — unifying the composition and adding action to the scene.

The *hangers* have it in the Bergdorf presentation of the three wood based suit forms with shoes on their shoulder and drooping wood *hanger* moustaches behind the flaunted ties. Matching pocket handkerchiefs are draped onto other *hangers* that appear over the shoulders like walnut wings. All that's missing are the *halos*. The trousers are neatly folded and stacked on the floor in front of the wood-turned bases.

In the Dunhill window it is the *hat racks* that do it. A Chorus Line of mahogany colored bentwood *hat racks* line up across the window and items of menswear are casually draped and carefully balanced on the many available *hooks*. Sitting on the ring that holds the unit together is a wooden artist's mannequin holding a card that discretely announces a sale in progress.

Alfred Dunhill, W. 50th St., NYC
George Shimko, Visual Director

Elizabeth Arden, Fifth Ave., NYC

H is for *harps* — *harpsichords* and *heart* and *harp-rendering* music. The antique silver finished *harp* is garlanded with vines of ivy while a gloved *hand* plucks away on the strings. Music fills the air — music sheets are everywhere; on the chair — on the floor — and on the stand where it belongs. The rear wall has sketched-on boiserie panels and is patterned with medallions gently lined in gold. The background is streaked with dripping paint and looks woefully aged and antique. To accompany the invisible *harpist,* the rigged suitforms have only to reach out for the cello and the violin on the splattered and leaf strewn floor. Let the concert begin.

Barneys, NY
Simon Doonan, Creative Director

Gucci, Fifth Ave., NYC
Guy Scarangello, Corp. Dir. of Visual Presentation

Hats go with *hat boxes* and *hat boxes* can also go with cosmetics, perfumes and assorted small fashion accessories. The piled up, striped black and white *hat boxes* echo the black and white diagonal stripe in the mannequins outfit. Black and white are also combined for the designer gloves and the *hat* she is wearing to crown her costume. One of the up front boxes is unlidded to reveal a flurry of white flowers and cascading green foliage which speaks for the season. The lighting in the display keeps the shopper on the street concentrated on the display rather than on the shop behind.

The Gucci *hat boxes,* also stripped in black and white, are arranged as a casual table rather than a studied build-up. The uppermost one is opened with a burst of orange tissue and a miniature black satin covered dressform is revealed beribboned and bedecked with a bottle of the precious perfume. On the various planes and plateaus leading up to the tissue explosion more toiletries are presented in easy clusters for viewing.

Bonwit Teller, Trump Tower, NYC
Frank Calise, SVM, Div. V.P. Store Design/V.M.

Saks Fifth Ave., NYC
Michael Keith, SVM, Div. V.P. Visual Merchandising

H is for *head gear* and that means *helmets* — *heraldic helmets* as worn by knights in armor — or sportspersons racing with danger in their plastic *helmets*. The three mannequins are wearing gleaming black plastic motorcycle head protectors to top off their sleek, stylish costumes in red and black leather. The floors and walls are deep charcoal gray and the sharp white lights reflect as brilliant balls of white on the black *helmets*. To complete the controlled red/black color scheme, the mannequins with pale almost white skins are wearing bright crimson lip make-up and sheer black hosiery with the black pumps.

H is for *hydrants* and *hydrants* usually are used to put out fires. In this DKNY display at Saks Fifth Avenue it can start a fashion fire with the Donna Karan designs in black and red. The flaming tressed mannequin near the *hydrant* and the mannequin layered in red sweaters are targeted for the fiery light from above while the white back wall is illuminated by the billboard fixtures hanging down in front of it. The fire *hydrant* is an urban symbol — it is seen on city streets and a single *hydrant* of a "cement" walk does a city street make — in display.

Chiquenaude, Montreal, Canada
Yves Guilbeault, Design
Andre Doyon, photographer

Horns begin with *H* — and no matter how they blow —
they can make a joyous sound — and make a pleasant
sight. The assorted *horns* are cut-out of foamcore and
detailed with artwork in black. They are arranged on a
black background — in a low lit and tightly lit window.
Bursting forth are scarves arranged to billow and flutter in
the blast of wind that has helped them to escape from
within the confining instruments. The same sort of thing
could be done with real band instruments which can be
borrowed from the local music store — or from a marching
band that isn't marching at the moment. It helps to have a
ceiling grid to suspend the instruments and carry the
floating and flying merchandise.

Gerry Goldblum, Toronto, Ont., Canada
Yves Guilbeault, Designer

I is for *instruments* and *instruments* make music. Music makes the world go round and makes seasons fly by on the wings of songs. There are: Spring Song — It Might As Well Be Spring — Spring Is Here — Summertime — In The Good Old Summertime — Summertime Love — Autumn Leaves and Autumn in N.Y. — F? 'ling Leaves — September Song — and the Christmas song book is without end. Real instruments, as shown on p. 97, or fun ones as shown here still help put music in your displays. The Classic display features black and white short formals and the environment is brilliant red. A make-believe cello adds its classic lines to those of the outfits on display and the miniature grand piano makes a grand contrast to the figures while it helps balance the display.

The ladies in red are getting their licks in for the holidays in their red-redder-reddest dresses and to help them stay in tune the music staff with the notes have been recorded on the front glass. The red floor board has been liberally sprinkled with gold glitter and sparkles aplenty.

Instruments can also be "medical" — "scientific" — "architectural" — "astronomical" and the right *instrument in the mannequin's hands can make her an instantly recognizable authority or professional. Many instruments* are available for the borrowing in exchange for a credit card.

Sonia Rykiel, Madison Ave., NYC
Marc Manigault, Designer

Gumps, San Francisco, CA
Robert Mahoney, SVM, Visual Director

I is for *inflatables* and these small, flat *items* can be filled with air to fill an area in the display window. Whether it is a dinosaur carrying a lace edged Mother's Day reminder as she daintily steps through a garden of miniature stone floral arrangements or they are brightly colored beach balls, balloons, rafts, floats — whatever, the *inflatables* start out small and soon loom up and take over. It is obvious the fun the displayperson can have with rubber duckies and other blow-ups for swimwear and beachwear or with helium filled balloons — securely tied down — for anniversaries, celebrations, sales, and New Year's Eve. If in doubt — blow one out!

I if for *irons* and *ironing boards* and that unlikely and by now unused twosome makes a unique prop-pair for jeweled costume jewelry and fancy trees. The *ironing board* raises them up and the iron keeps them down.

I is for *imagination* — and that is what this book is all about.

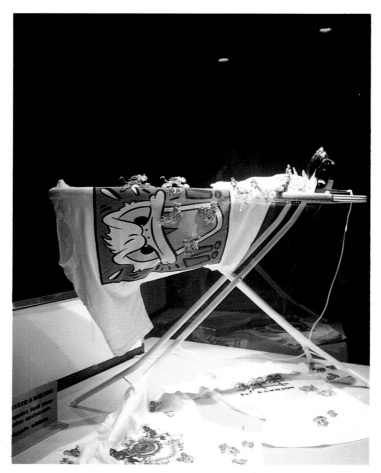

J is for *jelly beans* and they come in many flavors and as many colors. They can be used to fill candy *jars* and glass containers and coordinated with a color promotion — or just tossed or heaped in and about shoes, bags, belts and such. They are "sweet" — "delicious" and have even been given a presidential sanction. The Tiffany window carries the last letter of the message that began with L-O-V and together the four shadow box windows salute lovers, St. Valentine's day — and the gifts that go with the day.

J is for *jacks* and this *joint* is *jumping* with *jivin' jacks* — and the *jills* are dressed in a rainbow panorama of sun drenched colors. On pages 104-105, the Bendel window is alive with the razzamatazz of giant *jacks* flying high and lying low and the ball has bounced to the middle of the scene.

Butler & Wilson, S. Moulton St., London, England

Tiffany's, Fifth Ave., NYC
Gene Moore, Display Director

Pages 104-105: Henri Bendel, W. 57th St., NYC
Danuta Ryder, Visual Director

Jordan Marsh, Washington St., Boston, MA

106

Kitchens begin with *K* and *kitchens* are where the hearth is and where most days begin. It is where families meet and eat. It is table and chairs, refrigerators, stoves, microwave ovens, and — the *kitchen sink*. It is all those electric appliances in the warehouse/salesroom waiting to be invited to step in and become part of a window display. Jordan Marsh used the *kitchen* as an informal Christmas morning setting and it could certainly include a couple of kids in their sleepwear and bathrobes. Imagine what can be done with cereal boxes — with coffee and coffee makers for brown and beige promotions — with spices for red and gold themes — with cereal boxes. You can see what the red *ketchup* squeeze dispensers have done for the red and white men's sportswear display at Sakowitz. "For the flavor of ——." A career couple could start their morning over coffee in the *kitchen*. *Kids* carrying their lunch boxes or bags could be leaving for Back-To-School. It could even be a place to throw a party with the be-gowned and be-tuxed hostess and host carrying in the hors d'oeuvres and the chilled champagne. The contrast of costume to setting can be an effective attention getter. Imagine throwing open a refrigerator filled with fashion accessories — or a freezer overfilled with rhinestone jewelry and accessories. What can't you do with a microwave oven in a shadow box window when the accessories are hot. If you want it *kozy* or *kitch* — make it the *kitchen*.

Sakowitz, Houston, TX
Bob Fishburn, Corp. V.M. Director

K is for *kites* and *kites* fly high and wide from early spring through the summer skies with ribbon tails flapping behind. The Laura Ashley display uses simple paper kits in red and green to complement and go with the red summer dresses on the abstracts. The Bendel display is filled with the excitement and thrill of seeing the Summer sky all but blotted out by the hords of hundreds of soaring, dipping, floating, twisting and turning *kites*. These *kites* are all white as are the knotted and ribboned tails and the floor of the window. The walls are painted sky blue and most of the merchandise is white plus some gray and black with a single red jacket to make the statement. All the mannequins wear white cotton bandeaus on their wigless heads and dark, dark glasses. Could you see doing this window without a ceiling grid?

Laura Ashley, E. 57th St., NYC
Barbara Kleber, National V.M. Director

Henri Bendel, W. 57th St., NYC
Danuta Ryder, Visual Director

K is for *knights* and *knights-in-armor* are romantic. They recall "once upon a time" and "happily ever after," days of yore, men who are bold and damsels waiting to be rescued from dragons, ogres and towers. *Knights* stand for chivalry and heraldry and are seen in the company of Gothic arches, massive straight-lined thrones, lances and shields, tapestries and long banquet tables. *Knights* show up for Christmas and to accompany damsels in Medieval-inspired gowns encrusted with gold and colored stones or in vivid colored capes and wraps. If you can't get the *knight* — the armour will also do it.

Chapter 3

L

Lights — Lanterns — Lamps and Lampshades of all shapes and sizes — Legs, Limbs and left-over bits of worn out mannequins — Lambs in wooly coats — Ladders to lead the eye, to climb, to frame, to form into constructions — Leashes and Leads of Leather or chain to tie the mannequin to the doggie in the window — Lumber rough and ready to make a textural background or an abstract construction — Luggage with and without Labels to load up for holiday get-aways — Libraries stacked with books and accented with Ladders — Lattice of Lath — Lifesavers as nautical punctuation.

M

Monopoly — Mega-bucks and oversized paper Money — Moneybags to stuff with coins or dollars — Music, Musicians to play Musical instruments from Music sheets or ornate Music stands and Microphones to carry the tune — Mannikins and Mannequins used in unusual ways — Memorabalia, Memories and Mickey Mouse — Malls and Mallets — Mops and Moppets — Masks, Masques and Masked Balls — Magic — Magic tricks — Magicians — Miracles — Mirrors to reflect, to distort, to enhance.

N

The News and the Newspapers — Neon and Netting — Nautical and Navy.

O

Offices and Office furnishings; the desks, the files, the water fountain — Things that are Old, Out-of-date and Out-of-doors.

P

Paper Dolls — Papers, Pens and Pencils — Prisms and Prismatic colors — Parachutes to land with and to fill a window with sweeps of silk — Pictures, Portraits, Photos and Photographic equipment — Photocopies off the Press — Parties and Party-time with Party hats, Pinwheels, favors and Paper decorations — Panniers — Poufs — Portieres — Playing Cards — Paint, Paint Pans and Paint cans, Paint rollers and brushes, tubes of paint — Penguins in Pairs — Pennons and Pennants — Polo — Pom-Poms — things Provincial — Potatoes and Pumpkins — Pooches, Poodles and Pooper-Scoopers.

Woodward & Lothrop, Washington, DC
Jack Dorner, Div. V.P. of Visual Merchandising
Jan Suit, Washington V.M. Director

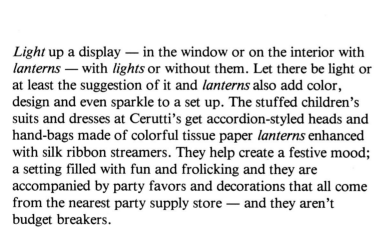

Cerutti, Madison Ave., NYC
Gaylord, Visual Director

Laura Ashley, E. 57th St., NYC
Barbara Kleber, National V.M. Director

Light up a display — in the window or on the interior with *lanterns* — with *lights* or without them. Let there be light or at least the suggestion of it and *lanterns* also add color, design and even sparkle to a set up. The stuffed children's suits and dresses at Cerutti's get accordion-styled heads and hand-bags made of colorful tissue paper *lanterns* enhanced with silk ribbon streamers. They help create a festive mood; a setting filled with fun and frolicking and they are accompanied by party favors and decorations that all come from the nearest party supply store — and they aren't budget breakers.

Laura Ashley's window is summer-*light* and the white akari *lanterns* — tissue stretched over a pliant bamboo frame — recalls by-gone parties on the lawn when people met, danced and romanced away a midsummer night's eve in civilized surroundings. The white transluscent globes also create a happy spatter-dash background for the polka-dot print presentation. At night, when the sunlight no longer competes with the threatrical display lamps, the 60 watt bulbs in the lanterns give off a gentle glow of illumination. *Lanterns* strung across an interior department could set that space off as something special.

You can't get much more elegant than the *lady* in red in the Elizabeth Arden window and her flaming gown is enriched by the matching color floor board and the red *lanterns* stenciled with gold at her feet. Red satin rosettes finish off the *lanterns*. *Looking for oversized ornaments for a Christmas display? Try the colored, ball-shaped lanterns —* with *lamps* inside them for a real holiday glow.

Elizabeth Arden, Fifth Ave., NYC
Walter Rummenie, Designer

Steven E., Great Neck, NY
Mindy Greenberg, Designer

Legs and *limbs* — and assorted body parts can be used in new ways to get across sometimes startling or shocking messages. At Steven E., there is a Wrap-Up Sale in progress and to underscore the message the body parts are wrapped in brightly colored gelatins or cellophane and tied up with equally strong colored twines. The anatomic assortment is arranged into an abstraction that would have made an early Picasso go green rather than blue at that period.

B. Altman found a new way to use old *legs* — and with a difference. A white frame is set onto a snow sprinkled floor and the *legs* are framed within the rectangle. A decorative dolly fashioned of fabrics and paper sculpture — all in white — reclines over the display of *legs* in the lastest in hosiery and footwear. The neutral gray backwall contrasts with the figure, frame and snow and sets off the black sheer hose and the stylish shoes.

Henri Bendel, W. 57th St., NYC
Danuta Ryder, Visual Director

B. Altman, Fifth Ave., NYC

Lambs begin with *L* and not only are they cuddly, cute and lovable — they are four-legged symbols for wool and warmth. Here, right out of the local toy store comes this herd of wooly *lambs* with black *legs* and muzzles — wandering aimlessly but with a purpose around the sweater clad mannequins in the Bendel window. Their aim is to point up the wool fibers used to make the assorted woven separates. *Lambs* also ask to be arranged wrapped in blankets to express comfort and warmth in a home furnishing display. When wool is the thing, allow the cuddly *lambs* to graze in the display areas and the shoppers will get the message.

Filene's, Boston, MA

Ladders are for climbing — for getting to the top — for vertical *lines* interrupted with horizontal dashes. *Ladders* can be drapers, hold merchandise in an ascending or descending arrangement. The rustic, rough-hewn *ladders* in the Filene "Country Weekend" window contrast with the fine panelled back wall but they do add an outdoor touch that complements the suedes, wools and jeans on the mannequins — meant for a country outing — and showing. A sweep of wool plaid fabric falls from a rung — softening the linear background while it backs up the brown suede and lambswool trimmed coat. The *lighting* has all the warmth and richness of an autumnal setting sun.

Marshall Fields, State St., Chicago, IL
Ken Smart, V.P. of Visual Merchandising
Jamie Becker, V.M. Director, State St. store

Sonia Rykiel, Madison Ave., NYC
Marc Manigault, Designer

L is for *leashes* — the long ribbons of *leather* or cotton or cord that *lead* the viewer's eye from the attention-getter (the doggie in the window) to the attention-making garment on the mannequin. Whether elegant and aloof, as in the Marshall Fields display where the well-mannered, silver-foiled pups are heeling and heeding — or confusing and confining as is the basset hound who is sniffing his way in and out of the red checkered threesome in the Sonia Rykiel window — the *leashes lead* the way and add humor to the situation. How much is that garment in the window? Follow the *lead* into the store and find out.

The Bloomingdale window has un-*leashed* a bronze beauty and the trio in white, yellow and fuchsia are trying to capture it — or at least share in its attention-winning popularity. Swags of brass chain serve as *leashes* as they swing back and forth across the black tiled floor, from the lithe sculpture on the marble tiled pedestal to the *ladies* clustered against the white wall flushed with pink light that surrounds them. The chains are wrapped about the three emphasizing how well they go together and the *leashes* lead the shoppers across the balanced composition.

Pages 118-119: Bloomingdales, Lexington Ave., NYC
Joe Feczko, SVM, V.P. of Visual Merchandising

M is for *Monopoly* and for *mega-bucks* — *money* and the *magnetic* appeal of oversized props in display situations. When you are playing to win, you just can't lose when the decoratives call out to the shopper on the street and invites them to come closer for a real look. Any number can play this game and the right moves include the placement of the props — the color coordination of the merchandise with the props and the lighting that picks out the next skip or jump. Nobody ever goes to jail here or goes bankrupt. AND — since *money* makes this game go round and round, proceed to the next page.

Henri Bendel, W. 57th St., NYC
Danuta Ryder, Visual Director

Luggage begins with *L* and so do most trips — vacations — voyages and scheduled departures. The cloud painted background at Bendel's and the cyclone fence suggest an airport or the entrance to a docked cruise ship. The *label* festooned and appliqued bags say it is "time for take-off" or to "sail-away" and the ladies are dressed to travel. The *luggage* also makes a convenient *ledge* for the *lady* to sit on because she doesn't know how long she has to wait.

L is for *lumber* and *lumber* constructs constructions like the one on p. 110. *L* is also for *libraries* and shelves filled with books and fashion accessories when it is time to say College, Career, Classic or Back to School. *Lattice* is made up of light *lath* strips criss-crossed into panels and dividers — waiting to be draped with ivy and garlands of flowers for garden settings. *Lampshades* (p. 146-7) don't just go on *lamp* bases when they can cover a mannequin's head or face for fun or shock appeal. *L* is also for *lifesavers* (p. 139) and they are for nautical settings and selling swimwear.

Alfred Dunhill, W. 50th St., NYC
George Shimko, Visual Director

At Dunhill's, the dress and suit forms are color coordinated to each other and the *leather luggage* on the floor. Whatever they can't wear they can pack and take with them so the coordinates and accessories are displayed on the bags that serve as effective risers.

M.G.A., Beverly Hills, Los Angeles, CA

Money-money-money — and it almost makes no difference what the color is so long as it looks like *money*. For a super Sale, Bendel's visuals designer left out all the *merchandise* and filled her window to overflowing with thousands and thousands of make-believe and not-so-make-believe *moola*. The paper stuff is gushing out of safes and vaults drawn with black lines on white foamcore. In addition, gold, silver and copper coins join in the exposition of *money* bursting forth from the partially opened containers. The front glass carries the message — *super sale*. In the adjacent small window the theme continues with a white canvas bag brimming over with all denominations of currency — bills and coins — and the crudely drawn $ is a caricature of the usual message stenciled on *moneybags*.

Henri Bendel, W. 57th St., NYC
Danuta Ryder, Visual Director

Bernard Perris, Madison Ave., NYC
Marc Manigault, Designer

Sherle Wagner, E. 57th St., NYC
Guy Kohn, Designer

Music also makes the world go round and the *musicians* are the *magicians* of sound. The Sherle Wagner display cleverly converts fabulous sinks into *musical instruments* and the African *masks* are attached to black and white striped log bodies. They are the *musical group* singing the wonders of their *merchandise* into *microphones* which are actually gilt plated fawcet handles mounted on metal rods. The red floor, the black and white canvas background with primitive artwork and the very naive and native *musicians* all contrast with the sleek, silver and gold fine finishes of the sink bowls.

Gucci, Fifth Ave., NYC
Guy Scarangello, Corp. Dir. of Visual Presentation

Play it again Sam-antha. And the song lingers on as the black *music staff* is applied onto the white wall where it shares space and the spotlights with the elevated shoes. The Gucci display also includes a *music stand* (see 202-3) which brings a black handbag up into eye-level prominence. The red/white/black color scheme is given an extra dash with the red squares under the stand and the black wiring snaking on it.

Lord & Taylor, Fifth Ave., NYC
Alan Petersen, SVM, V.P. of Visual Merchandising

Sheets of *music* make a melodious and *monochromatic* background for the straw hat riding in on a blast of brass. The Lord and Taylor shadow box is scaled to please and the *music sheets* say "Spring Song — Easter Bonnet" or they will provide the melody for any season or almost any garment from the daring Lady in Red to the demure one in her Alice Blue Gown.

M is for *memorabilia* and that includes the flying daredevils of the 30's — *mannequins* that mirror another time and place — and the ageless *Mickey Mouse*. It is for the *memories* of the 40's and 50's and the Good Old Days. Macy's Aeropostale window (p. 126) is full of symbols that are not too antique but old enough to bring a freshness to the new fashions that echo the styling of the by-gone era. The window is aclutter with bits and pieces of the 30s and 40s when barn-storming was a way of life for the hardy few. Today the masses can relive those exciting moments by dressing in the clothes inspired by them. There is also a wealth of textures introduced that say *masculine* or *manly*.

The ladies with *Mickey Mouse* on p. 127 are also sharing the display space with *memorabilia* — the *music makers* and entertainment centers of the 50's; the juke box and the mini-screened T.V. sets that heralded the way to the future.

Lane Bryant, NYC
Vincent Milan, Dir. of Visual Merchandising, Fifth Ave.

Macy's, Herald Square, NYC

Macy's, Herald Square, NYC

M is for *mannekins* — *mannikins* or *mannequins* but large or small — life-size or *miniature* — made of wood, plastic or papier mache — these articulated figures offer a world of display opportunities beyond wearing or showing off the garments. In the *masked* down Macy's shadow box the *mannikins* are used to pack a bag with accessories-to-go while another *mannikin* has shinnied up the pole to check out the flow of fashionable watches down to the receiving bag. These artist's helpers can and will assume most human positions and they are scaled to please. They are small enough to play up fashion accessories and when used with dressed full size *mannequins* they become the Lilliputians ready to climb-up, scamper-up or be hoisted-up to help dress and accessorize the modern-day Gulliver or Gulliveress.

Barneys, Seventh Ave., NYC
Simon Doonan, Creative Director

Alfred Dunhill, W. 50th St., NYC
George Shimko, Visuals Director

M is for *mallets* and *mallets* are for more than polo. They suggest outdoor activities, a place in the sun, fun and games with a sense of style and class. In this presentation at Alfred Dunhill the *mallets* are used to introduce and interact with the wide bands of belting. The pattern made by the assembled *mallets* makes a most pleasing composition that scores with the viewer.

Mops and *moppets* go together when it is clean-up time in pinafores made of polka dots and checks. The rear wall is grafitti-ed with tic-tac-toe markings and the *mannequins* are white washed to better show off the black/red prints highlighted with white. The *mops* are for cleaning up — for adding lines to the composition that direct the viewer but they could be equally effective for sale promotions when shoppers *clean-up* values. The kerchief head-dresses add humor to the *mopping moppets* at Barneys.

Henri Bendel, W. 57th St., NYC
Danuta Ryder, Visual Director

Masks and *masques* begin with *M* and go to *mardi-gras* and *masquerades*. Whether they are stocking *masks* or elegant ball *masques* or harlequin *masks* or dominos they do add *mystery* and suspense and a feeling of carnival to a presentation. In the Bendel display, the *mannequins* are *masked* with strands of colored wool yarns — like unraveling stocking *masks* or balaclavas that never got knitted at all. More yarn is wrapped around hands like *mittens* and around feet like socks all to emphasize the hand knitted warmers worn by the semi-realistic *mannequins* with the yarns at top. See p. 218.

For going to a *masked ball,* the Saks Fifth *mannequin* is revealed in all her fur and finery splendor. The gilt chair is all it takes to set the scene, the *mask* painting behind echoes the black and white of the *merchandise* presented. The red ambience lights the fire. She carries a gilded face *mask* on a beribboned rod.

At Bergdorf's they are stretching a point to make the point. The ladies in lovely lingerie are going incognito but their is nothing hidden about the garments they are wearing. Lace edged fabric is shaped into harlequin *masks* and the excess fabric is rolled and attached to the rear wall; a most unusual effect and definitely an eye-catcher.

On pages 132-133 are more *masks*. These papier mache caricatures are used to create interest in the realistic mannequins standing in their midst.

Saks Fifth Ave., NYC
Michael Keith, SVM, V.P. of Visual Merchandising

Bergdorf Goodman, Fifth Ave., NYC
Angela Patterson, V.P. Dir. of Store Design/V.M.

Pages 132-133: Complex Desjardines, Montreal, Que.
Yves Guilbeault, Designer
Andre Doyon, photographer

The Fur Vault, Seventh Ave., NYC
Anthony Nardi, Visuals Director

Magic and *miracles* begin with *M* and usually they are pure illusion. Whether it is a mannequin suspended in mid-air — being sawed in half — or cards flying in space, it is what the viewer perceives and not what she sees. The designer at the Fur Vault has pulled a few tricks out of his hat or from up his sleeve to create the *magic show* in the windows featuring the store's remodeling and storage services. The easel up front announces "the act" and the red draped proscenium *masks* the window and turns the black space into the stage. The viewer wants to believe that fur-coated figure is suspended between the neon colored hoops and she ignores the fine lines that are holding up the cards that are part of the bow-tied *magician's* trick. *Magic* is a top hat — a wand — bunnies and doves to pull out of the hat or the unending stream of colorful kerchiefs — or *merchandise* rising from the hat. *Magic is mystery* and *mystery* is believing what one isn't seeing — and that is illusion.

Barneys, Seventh Ave., NYC
Simon Doonan, Creative Director

M is for *mirrors* where you sometimes see what you don't want to believe. *Mirrors* on the wall — *mirrors* that stand on the floor or hold in your hand always, in display, answer that "fairest in the land" question with the merchandise currently on view. The elegant gilt pier or cheval *mirror* of antique design like the white sun glass pompadour wig recall the late 18th century French court and the black velvet ribbon striped back wall adds class while it repeats the ribbon motif that wraps around the pale mannequin. The back wall is blushing pink and the figure stands in a pool of white light.

To carry out a contemporary circus theme, the very stylish dress is shown in front of a convoluted "Fat/Skinny" mirror that brings back childhood memories of fun houses — carnivals and side-shows. Though the reflection is warped — the actual garment wins by comparison and the shopper does get to see another angle of the outfit.

Hugo Boss, Washington, DC

Newspapers are all about what is *new* and what is happening. *Newspapers* come in different prints — in different languages — but they all tend to say the same things. They are black on white and gray all over; perfectly *neutral* and a perfect prop for things timely.

At Hugo Boss the shiny black abstracts have read all about it in their papers — "a Wall St. Take Over" — and they're now waiting for the revelation which will come when the *newspaper* shrouded mannequin is unwrapped and revealed in a stock-rising outfit. This inexpensive prop — the *newspaper* (even one a few days old) — provides something for the form to hold as well as a suspenseful covering.

In the Sloane St. window in London these forms are informed and up to the minute in what's hot — and where to get it. They not only have the pulse of it — they are the market. One form is topped with a rolled up paper while the arms are rigged to hold another. The other form is involved with the phone to verify the *news*. On the floor — neatly folded sheets of *newsprint* serve as accent blocks for the accessories and to provide a pattern on the *natural* wood floor.

Macy's San Francisco has taken the paper into the vignette version of a high power office setting and has "upholstered" and upgraded an everyday common office chair into a seat of importance. The attache case is natural leather but another all-important *newspaper* lies on the floor. The all black setting is dramatized by a blast of red light on the chair in the *news* while the mannequin stands in a glow of his own.

Men's Shop, Sloane St., London

Macy's, San Francisco, CA

136

Macy's, Herald Square, NYC

Ungaro, Madison Ave., NYC
Marc Manigault, Designer

N is for *neon* and *netting* and in this Macy's display for Soprani menswear the *neon* and *net* are combined for a startling and electrifying effect. A wiggle of red neon light wends its way through the display; from the floor up across the threesome to the un-handed form/figure on the left. More bent *neon* tubes, unilluminated, criss cross over the group with their shiny chicken wire mesh heads and hands. Even their shoes are made of the same metallic net. The outfits are worn with white tee shirts emblazoned with the Luciano Soprani name and the clear white beams of light pass through all that red illumination to show off the designer's name. How exciting can a display get? Check this one out for light — for diagonal lights — and for the shocking and surprising details.

For a shipboard romance it does take a *nautical* setting with *N* as in *nautical, naughty* and *navy*. These well dressed women are sitting it out in the merest suggestion of the fabulous cruise ship or ocean liner they are on. Portholes are sketched onto the front glass as are the stylized, chevron shaped waves below. The only dimensional objects used are the white and natural wood railing up front with the lifesaver attached and the deck chair for the seated figure. Behind, in this open backed window is the grill that closes off the display area from the store at night. The ''sun'' is bright at sea and that makes the dark glasses a must fashion accessory.

Kaufmanns, Pittsburgh, PA
David Knouse, V.P. of Visual Merchandising
Anthony Lucas, Downtown V.M. Director

O is for *office* and *office equipment* and the *office* can be a setting for career-oriented fashions for men and women. As the reader peruses this book, he and she will find settings suggested by a chair (see p. 137), a desk, an easel with a lamp. The men in the Saks window are successful because they are dressed for success. The traditional boiserie of the rear wall is painted white and carries a single framed architectural detail drawing. A charcoal gray painted stool and the sleek black and chrome hi-tech drafting table under the dropped white metal lamp dress the set and the viewer can fill in the rest. The drawings (see blueprints) make good reading and they provide a central focal point for the composition; this is where the men gather together and the action is natural and realistic. The "client" is wearing a jacket and carries a drawing while his expensive attache case rests at his feet. The more casual pair must be the architects or designers.

The old, battered and often bruised and neglected old wood desk moves *out* of the *office* to *out-of-doors* for a unique picnic setting. Summer living is the theme — and the living is easy. The designers have cast aside the symbols of work like the adding machine, typewriter and telephone and they've turned the desk into an elevated surface decorated with checkered cloths to show off the color coordinated picnic wares. The desk chair has been replaced by a sun-deck chair and a pair of sneakers are waiting to be stepped into. The back wall is painted sky-blue highlighted with fluffy white clouds.

Office files are also great props waiting to be pulled open to reveal fashion accessories or garments properly filed away under S for Shoes — J for Jewelry — N for New.

Saks Fifth Avenue, NYC
Michael Keith, SVM, V.P. of Visual Merchandising

Elizabeth Arden, Fifth Ave., NYC
Walter Rummenie, Designer

Alexanders, NYC
Sal Marra, Director of Design and Store Planning

P is for *parachutes* which can land in the window in a sweep of silk. At Bendel's the message reads — Land Feet First and the accent is on the hosiery. This is another grand and glorious way to use legs only in an imaginative manner to play up the always important fashion accessories of leg coverings and shoes. The billowing white silk *parachutes* cover the upper part of this extra tall window and the legs are floating down in a maze of guy lines and supports. The X on the dark floor indicates the landing spot and the lamps set across the front glass and side wall guides the *parachutists* to the place. If you can't borrow the chutes, try making them of bed-sheets or the bleached muslin that is 108'' wide and can be cut into big circles easily and with enough white cords — nobody will notice they are erzatz.

Bendels, W. 57th St., NYC
Danuta Ryder, Visual Director

P is for *paper* — *pens* and *pencils* — *prisms* and *prismatic colors.* The Elizabeth Arden loungewear is shown in bright crayon *pencil* colors. The Night Matches are matched to the strong *prismatic* rods that are the overscaled *pencils.* The helter-skelter effect of criss crossed *pencils* provides a sense of excitement and the dramatic play of color is heightened by the fuchsia floor board and the red/orange wigs on the mannequins. *Pencils* make a *point* or they *point* it out if it isn't too obvious.

What is obvious is that it is Back To School time when one sees the kids in the Alexander's window with the *pencil,* ruler and assorted world globes that add to the seasonal look. Note the composition of lines; the *pencil* brings the eye to the ruler — the ruler runs down to the floor and to the globes that roll on over to the boy. His red sleeve goes back to the vertical unit in the middle — and the *pencil* — and it starts all over again.

Bertolini, Ste. Catherine St., Montreal, Que.

Pictures — portraits — photos — and *photographic paraphernalia* all begin with *P* and can put the mannequin or form into the fashion *picture*. The semi abstracts in the Bertolini window are inundated by and also quite unphased by the *photographic equipment* they are sharing space with. The shiny silver *photo lamps* and the reflector umbrellas and camera cases that clutter up the floor all suggest a fashion shoot. Chairs are set about and used as elevations for coordinates and accessories. The models are lined up behind — cool, calm, coordinated and ready to be *pictured* on a front cover.

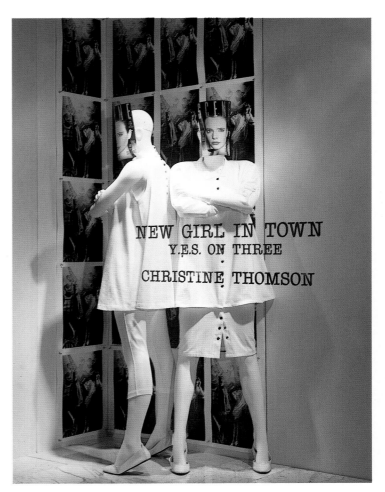

Bloomingdales, NYC

Right off the *press* — hot and stylish — and the *pictures* on the magazine covers become masks for the white abstract mannequins in white — in the all-white setting. In the corner, behind, black and white *prints* or *photo-copies* — reproduced from the magazine show off how current the fashions are.

Charles Jourdan, Trump Tower, NYC

The *picture* has been taken and copies are made by the dozens — mounted and cut out and stacked on the gray cube build-ups in the Jourdan window. The bust of the lady in dark glasses features a black gloved hand holding a red slipper and her coat is a red/black houndstooth pattern. On the mounting steps up is shown a variety of mostly red and black shoes and bags with a few purple ones for accents.

It's *party-time* on pages 146-147. It is time to dress up in *portieres* — be pampered with *poufs* and to pander to the wild urge to wear a lampshade and a table top as a *pannier*. This Barneys men's formal wear window is wicked and delightfully surrealistic. Up front the suit forms are beautifully rigged in formal wear and the coordinates and accessories are sedately presented but behind is madness and the making of the *party* of the season. The lady on the left is busy on the *phone* and she's using *playing cards* as *place cards* for the *phormal* occasion.

Pages 146-147: Barneys, Seventh Ave., NYC
Simon Doonan, Creative Director

The Limited, Madison Ave., NYC
Michael Hickson, Reg. Presentation Coordinator

P is for *paper* — all kinds of *paper* from *wrapping paper* to gift wrap *presents* — to seamless or no seam *paper* in long, unending rolls — to *notebook papers* and *papers* of all colors and textures that seem to go for all seasons, *promotions* and *presentations*.

Taking advantage of the two story high window, the design team at The Limited combined kraft wrapping *paper* with twine and wrapped up an Earth Tone *promotion* by covering floor, wall and assorted dress forms with the crushed, crumpled, beige *paper*. Forms were elevated for a series of eye levels and outfits as well as accessories were *presented* on the *paper* covered forms.

Using a range of monochromatic seamless *papers* from white to black with grays in between the rolls of *paper* became a *pipe organ* behind the dressed forms in the foreground. One roll of *paper* makes a slash around the collection of *paper boxes* and bags grouped around the draped pant legs. Using gold or silver foil *papers* could make *pipes* to fill a Christmas display with the sound of carols.

Paper dispensers and waste *paper* baskets are familiar objects but when the dispenser yields unending folded maps that zig zag out of the white enameled containers — that is different and a unique setting for luggage and/or *portmanteaus* on the go. Trunks, satchels and bags are open — revealing more maps and even the waste *paper* basket is filled with crushed and crumpled maps. A great way to get up and go.

Alfred Dunhill, W. 50th St., NYC
George Shimko, Visuals Director

149

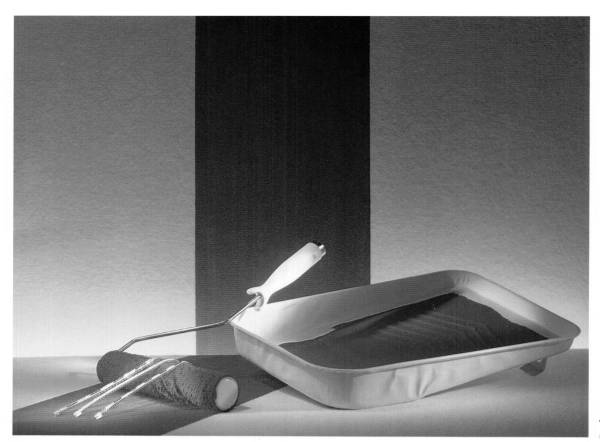

Tiffany's, Fifth Ave., NYC
Gene Moore, Design Director

Marshall Fields, State St., Chicago, IL
Ken Smart, V.P. of Visual Merchandising
Jamie Becker, State St. V.M. Director

P is for *paint* — *paint pans* and *cans* — *paint rollers* and *brushes* and for *presenting promotions* with color and flair. The exquisite bracelets set with diamonds and rubies get a spectacular and unexpected sendoff on the red swath of *paint* and the matching dyed *roller* that holds them. The red ribbon of *paint* runs down the rear wall and leads to the white handle of the *roller* and to the *pool* of bright light on the bracelets in the Tiffany window. The shadow box technique could be used for small fashion accessories of any color.

Painting begins with *P* and whether the *portrait* is the original or just a *print,* a *picture* can make a statement. The Napoleonic code is getting a splashy showing in this Marshall Fields men's window with the tri-colored flag or *pennon* or *pennant* blowing in the *prints*. On the front glass is drawn the outline of an ornate frame that encompasses the black abstract figure as well as the wall arrangement of gilt frames on the red flocked *wallpaper* background.

150

Kaufmanns, Pittsburgh, PA
David Enouse, V.P. of Visual Merchandising
Anthony Lucas, Downtown V.M. Director

Polo and *porch* both begin with *P* — *polo* as *played* on a horse — or by wearing one on one's chest. This setting brings together a *paint*-stained, weathered *porch, provincial paraphernalia* and the traditional dress forms one associates with *polo* merchandise. *Plants* grow in the foreground and *pine* trees and shrubs add credence to the *Polo* Country stenciled on the window. Red and pink lights supply depth and dimension to the scene.

Party decorations and *party favors* begin with *P* and end as fun. Here, using easy to procure *props* and pieves is a Fourth of July summer window with a *pinwheel* or red/white/blue hanging overhead from a ceiling grid and Uncle Sam top hats *(party hats) parade* down the red and blue covered runways along with assorted white shoes. The hats serve as *platforms* — as breaks in the flow of shoes. The Uncle Sam figure is the central focal point that connects the *pinwheel* above with the assembled shoes below.

Elizabeth Arden, Fifth Ave., NYC
Walter Rummenie, Designer

Paper dolls are cut-outs with a memory. They repeat the same design over and over again as they zig zag back and forth carrying with them also fond memories of childhood when cutting out the *paper dolls* took the place of watching T.V. There is also a naive charm associated with them. They are easy to make — easy to use and with some *planning* — they can be multicolored or alternating figures can still be linked together. Size is optional; stiff paper like construction *paper* will work for smaller sizes used as swags or garlands but up to lifesize ones can be cut out of cardboard or foamcore then joined hand to hand — foot to foot to stand like an accordion pleated fence of figures. The big ones can wear clothes — or show off fashion accessories.

Paper bags — especially those with the store's name *printed* on them are always useful in displays as witnessed in the Elizabeth Arden Sale window. The up-scaled bags impart an up-graded image to a Sale presented with taste and class. The white artwork door behind "opens" into the store where the event is taking place.

Jildor, Cedarhurst, NY

OPE
SUNDA
12 -

MGA, Beverly Hills, Los Angeles, CA

Sonia Rykiel, Madison Ave., NYC
Marc Manigault, Designer

P is for *penguins* and *pairs* and one of the most popular fashion *pairing* is Black and White and nothing seems to say black and white with as much charm as *penguins* made of *plastics, papier mache* or puffed-up inflatables. In the Rykiel window the stylized mannequins are complemented by the stylized *penguins* with their *pearl* studded shirt fronts and red satin bow ties. They form a chorus line across the front glass line as *precise* and orderly as the Rockettes — in contrast to the back and forth movement of the mannequins behind them.

Poms-poms are just shredded *paper* but what spirit and *pow*! they can instill in a Back to College or Casuals *promotion*. It's a rah-rah — go get 'em feeling and when the background and floor are grass green marked off in yards of white — anything that's on *parade* is sure to make a touchdown and score heavily. To go with the *poms-poms* there could be school *pennants* and these cheerleaders have megaphones to carry the message out to the crowd. This display will make one for the old gipper — and be a boost for fall business for men, women and the kids. You can't lose especially when you play up the colors of the home team or the local school or college.

I. Miller, Fifth Ave.
Howard Nevelow, Designer

Henri Bendel's, W. 57th St., NYC
Danuta Ryder, Visuals Director

One *potato* — two *potato* — *pumps* and cut-outs — the *potatoes* are a contrast to the snakeskin shoes and bags and they're neutral in color. The unexpected spud makes an impression as it elevates the shoes on a bumpy surface off the green floor board.

Bendel welcomes fall and Halloween with a crop of big, bright orange *pumpkins* and the un-bumpkin like ladies are beautifully dressed in black velvet and white silk coordinates with wide brimmed hats and gloves as fashion accessories. The *pick*-of-the-crop *pumpkins* are also accessorized; their stems are ornamented with sassy black velvet bows and they bask in the orange/gold light. The white wall behind is washed with cool blue light and some of the warm light that touches the *pumpkins* spills on to the wall and turns in lavender.

P is for *poodles* and *prohibitive signs* — and *pooper scoopers* for those who can't or won't read the signs. The *park* setting has to be urban and the ladies are walking their raffia *poodle* along the cork gravel path that cuts through the green grass lawn covered with daisies. The blue sky behind gets bluer with the backwall lighting and the clouds are barely visible. The black and red coordinates are accessorized with gold "coin" belts and costume jewelry. Even the *pooch* is wearing a jeweled choker.

Barneys, Seventh Ave., NYC
Simon Doonn, Creative Director

Chapter
4

Q Quilts patched and unpatched — Quails and feathered tails.

R Racing, Racing stripes, colors, cars and flags — Ribbons tied and untied — Rosettes of Ribbon nice and pretty — Ropes of cotton, sisal or hemp for nautical wrap-ups or clothesline hang-ups — Rakes — Rugs oriental for traveling or otherwise.

S Stairs and Steps for rising up or laying down — Snow, Snowmen, Snowflakes and Snow sprites — Sleds and Sleighs to ride the Snow — Shutters and Suburbia — Swatches, Scraps, Strips and Skins stretched or collaged — Safaris with Spears, Shields, animal Skins and Straw wrapped drums — Sailing, Sailboats, Sails, Sailors and Sailor hats — Seaworthy Seagulls — Statues and Statuary — Scrim and Screening — Screens as backgrounds in open back windows — Swings and Strings of lights — Star filled Skies and patriotic Sales — Sticks for tossing — Shoelaces for tying — Surfs for riding on Surfboards — Sea, Sun and Sand — Skates and Skateboards — Shavers and Sinks.

T Tires and Treads and Inner Tubes — T.V. sets with stories to tell — Trombones and Tubas to play up musical Themes — Telephones, Telephone directories and Telephone wires to tie in with Teen-Agers — Tuxedos and Top Hats for dress-up occasions — Tapes and Tapemeasures for made-to-order occasions — Tassels — Targets — Theater, Theatrical posters and settings — Travel on a Tricycle — Take off on a Tryke — Tripods and Tricornes.

U Underwater and Undersea — Umbrellas for rain or shine anywhere in the Universe.

Lord & Taylor, Fifth Ave., NYC
Alan Petersen, SVM, V.P. of Visual Merchandising

Pages 160-161: Macy's, Herald Square, NYC

NEW YORK SPORT

ANDRA RHODES

R is for *racing* — *racing flags* — *racing stripes* — *race cars* and *raceways* for them to run around on. On p. 158 and 160-161 there are some suggestions of how these elements can be combined with the right merchandise into prize winning displays — good to the last lap. On a *raceway* that wended its *roller-coaster* way through a run of windows, the miniature *racers* zoomed in and out of presentations of black, white and red striped and patterned pieces while the accessory shadow box (p. 158) carried through on the theme. It is the final flag — the black and white checkered one — that signals it's trophy-time on p. 160-161, and the assemblage of black/white/yellow garments in the Macy's window can't lose no matter how they are mixed or matched.

Barneys, Seventh Ave., NYC
Simon Doonan, Creative Director

Henri Bendel, W. 57th St., NYC
Danuta Ryder, Visual Director

Bergdorf Goodman, Fifth Ave., NYC
Richard Currier, Dir. of Visual Presentation

R if for *ribbons* — streamers of silk, satin, grosgrain, tafetta or cotton. These long, seemingly endless strands can be dropped from above as a step-through curtain for a mannequin making an entrance, or criss crossed in a contrasting color against a wall to become a lattice design with snippets of the *ribbon* used as floor scatter, or carefully lined up from ceiling to floor and then across to the window with other *ribbon* streamers weaving between them at right angles for a sharp, precise plaid. *Ribbons* come in many colors and widths and are sometimes printed with designs or special logos. Uncut lengths of designer labels make very up-scaled streamers for the designer's clothes. Black velvet *ribbon* is always chic and special (see p. 135). Ribbon bows can be applied against the front glass (p. 160) or the display designer can snare the mannequins by enmeshing them in a maze of *ribbon* strands that turn the space into a spider's web gone mad and with no *rhyme* or *reason* except it also gets the viewer's eye and keeps it captive — and captivated.

Bergdorf Goodman, Fifth Ave., NYC

RIEDEL

Rosettes are *ribbons* with a *reason*. They are the award winning designators — the *ribbons* flutter that gets attached to prize winners — to leaders — to things that are judged the winner — or who place and show. The Gucci display *reveals riding* boots and *riding* habits — and for the "horsey set" a poster for a classic *riding* event. The rich *ribbon rosettes* makes winners of them all — gives them status and makes them worthy of being exhibited like prize winning artwork or craft pieces.

R is for *rakes* and *rakes* are for *raking* in fall leaves or, as in this set-up, *ribbon* decorated fall shoes. The common everyday garden-variety *rake* adds dynamic diagonals to the composition as it brings some of the shoes from eye level down to the floor where the main clustering of shoes is located. A brilliant spot on the *red* shoes and floor burns a hole in the middle of the display which, in turn, casts a fiery glow over the rest of the merchandise on the neutral gray floor.

167

Henri Bendel, W. 57th St., NYC
Danuta Ryder, Visual Director

Sonia Rykiel, Madison Ave., NYC
Marc Manigault, Designer

Rope them in — tie them down — brand them and never let them get away. *Cotton rope* — *sisal rope* — or *clothesline rope* — they are all different and all the same. The main difference is size. For imports, travel, for hoisting in crates, cartons and unloading the new arrivals — it takes strong, sturdy, sisal *rope* as illustrated in the Bendel display. Its massive scale and seeming weight carry along a feeling of power that contrasts with the pretty, pastel, flowery prints on the gently flowing fabrics.

The cotton *rope* is "yo-ho-ho" and away to the sea we go for things natural and nautical. It just as naturally teams up with sailor hats, life savers, and deck-swabbing mops. For red/white/blue promotions — for navy presentations — scatter the stars and twist the outfits in cotton *rope* like they did at Sonia Rykiel.

Wash and wear is still here — and clotheslines will always be accepted where garments are washed or rinsed and hung up to dry. Whether the *rope* is snarled and tangled and teamed up with wash baskets or soap and water filled pails — or pulled taut across the display area and clothespin hung with scarves, swim suits, infant's wear or separates — the clothes line is a cliche that says, "It takes to water" — "Easy to care for."

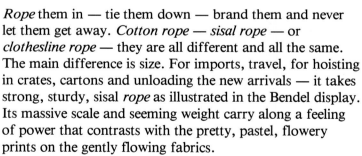

Kaufmann, Pittsburgh, PA
David Knouse, V.P. of Visual Merchandising
Anthony Lucas, Downtown, V.M. Director

S is for *sleds* and *snow* and *shutters* and *suburbia*. The fine men's leather shoes, cases, belts and bags are shown against the weathered door and *shuttered* panels. The *sled* serves to elevate some of the shoes and the snappy suspenders are unfurled across the door. A welcome mat — the *symbol* of hospitality — is set out on the brick *step* which is touched by and surrounded with *snow*.

Cole-Haan, Madison Ave., NYC
David Julin/Scott Larabee, Designers

S is for *stairs* which are *steps* that are *stepping up* or *out*. They provide measured elevations that tread *step by step* to bring merchandise from one viewing point to the next. The *stair railing* and *steps* in the Lord & Taylor menswear display are part of the "country estate" vignette *setting* which includes books, provincial furniture and a wheat and *straw* filled wooden cannister. On the *steps* are fashion coordinates, shoes on books, and the raised *suit form* sits on the uppermost *step* and the trousers drape down over them. This is a *super suburban scene* with *style*.

The rough hewn *steps* in the H.A.E. Smith display of fine Italian leather bags contrast the elegant *skins* against the rough *surface* of the wood and the *smooth stones* on the floor. Note the care and balance that went into the arrangement of the *stones* piled up on the bags — filling in the *spaces* between bag and *step* or where the wood has been chipped out of the vertical *support*. The exquisite lighting plays texture against texture and the merchandise wins out.

Swatches — *scraps* — *strips* and *skins* all begin with *S* — as do *scarves* and *stretchers*. On pages 172-173 we show interesting backgrounds using these *S*-inspired ideas. The Bergdorf ladies are backed up by a *sophisticated* collage of *swatches* of wallpaper, *scraps* of stitched fabrics and small *scarves* of assorted patterns. The Macy semi-abstracts or *stylized* mannequins are wearing the popular animal prints and to add an authentic touch striped and spotted *skins* are *stretchered* on simple wood frames tied with raffia. *Spears*, *shields* and native drums complete the *safari setting*.

H.A.E. Smith, Hamilton, Bermuda
Wm. H. Collieson, Visual Director

Bergdorf Goodman, Fifth Ave., NYC

Pages 174-175: Scoring with the scoreboard at Macy's, Herald Square, NYC

MINUTES SE

PERIOD
Fair-Play

HOME VI

Sonia Rykiel, Madison Ave., NYC
Marc Manigault, Designer

S is for *statues* and there is no *status* more dear to the *American spirit* than the *Statue of Liberty* and all she stands for. Standing or seated, it is the tiara and torch that people recognize and here is a loving and respectful take-off on the lady in an all black/white setting to complement the merchandise of the same contrasting couple at MGA. The rear wall is filled with positive and negative *stats* of the *statue* and the tile patterns cover the floor and cube the mannequin rests on. Her "torch" is more contemporary and hi-tech than the lady's traditional one but it does shine brightly. The blonde's face is mostly hidden by the inexpensive plastic tiarra/mask from the fun store that has been sprayed black for this occasion.

S is for *sailing — sail boats — sailors — sailor's hats.* It is for *sale* events — *special promotions.* Red is always a *season*ally successful color at Sonia Rykiel and in perusing this book the reader can see many clever ways of reintroducing the ever popular red. In this Rykiel window the red coordinates go to *sea* in a red and white striped *sail boat.* They are wearing their *sailing hats* and holding on to the big *ship model* by a cotton rope that snakes its way through the presentation area. Black and white are used to accent and accessorize the outfits and on the front glass a flock of *sea gulls* swoop and soar — *simply* rendered in yellow paint.

The *seaworthy* twosome at Alfred Dunhill are wearing their Navy jackets over white trousers lashed at the bases with belts. White cotton ropes are slung over the well rigged *suit forms* and the floor is awash with white *sailor* hats — dozens of them. The really delightful touch here that the viewers will remember are the "waves" that swoosh around the hats; they are spring clothespins clipped onto one another and shaped to form the rolling surf.

Alfred Dunhill, W. 50th St., NYC
George Shimko, Visual Director

MGA, Beverly Hills, Los Angeles, CA

S is for *scrim* and for *screens* and *screening* — the fine metallic mesh that can take on a *silky* softness and slithery suppleness as used in this Gucci display of subtle suede outfits. The use of colored lights is extraordinary and turns the silvery finish from red to blue to lavender depending upon how the theatrical lights hit the reflective *surface*. The mannequins are carefully picked out with sharp mini-spots on their faces and chests — just enough to *show* off the colors of the outfits.

Henri Bendel, W. 57th St., NYC
Danuta Ryder, Visual Director

Bloomingdales, Lexington Ave., NYC
Joe Feczko, SVM, V.P. of Visual Merchandising

Swings start with *S* and *swings* sweep through a *space* raising mannequins and merchandise to new and assorted heights. Each new height creates a new eye level and the change of viewing level adds a uniqueness and *special* quality to the garment featured. In the Bloomingdale's display the walls are upholstered in white as are the seats of the *swings* and the cotton roping that *suspends* them from above. The beige and white costumes are shown together but each gets a viewing *separate* but yet part of the same composition.

For Christmas lingerie the white wigged mannequins at Bendels take to the *swings* and the *swings* take full advantage of the extra high ceiling. Interspersed between the different levels of *swings* are dozens and dozens of *strings* of white bee lights that add thousands of points of light to this celebration of sleepwear.

Gucci, Fifth Ave., NYC
Guy Scarangello, Corp. Dir. of Visual Presentation

179

Bally, Ste Catherine St., Montreal, Que.

Athletic Style, W. 57th St., NYC

S is for *sticks* — for picking up or dropping down — for *scattering* through a display space — for *special* constructions that raise merchandise off the ground and yet keep them in the total design composition. The diagonal lines underscore the exciting quality of the colorful shoes and the green wall and floor complement the primary red, yellow and blue of the *sticks* in *space*.

Shoelaces hang from the ceiling grid to make a frolicking free feeling for the sneakers attached to them. The sharp colored streamers and ribbons add to the light-hearted quality of the already technicolored footwear as they unite them all into a memorable arrangement. The *shoelaces* could be ribbons and many other small fashion accessories could be dangling in this sort of display — if there is a ceiling grid to attach them to.

S is for *surf* — *surfing* — *surfboards* also *skate boards* and *skates* — roller or ice. These are the *symbols* of youth — of *sun-stained* gods and goddesses on California beaches where *sea* and *surf* and whitecaps reign supreme. For colorfilled casual and/or Hawaiian-style *sports* clothes — a *surfboard* or *skateboard* is sure to put the action into Activewear. In the Macy's window the floor is covered with *sand* which goes with *sea* and *surf*. The red flippers are a fashion accessory with flair.

S is for *safari* — for jungle adventurers — for hunting out the right fashions to wear to the tropics or on a Caribbean cruise.

Snow — *snowflakes* — and *snow sprites* all start with *S* and so does *Swan Lake* if fur coats are being shown with tutus in *snowy settings*.

For Father's Day remember *S* as in *sink* — *shave* — and *soap* whether it is for the little *shaver shaving* off the *soap* in front of the mirror over the *silk* — or the big guy looking for his *shaving supplies*. The *silk/shaving* setting is a natural for all that nice smelling stuff that people like to give and get. Remember — the ultimate prop is — ''everything but the kitchen *sink*.''

Macy's, NYC

T is for *tires* — *treaded* or re-treaded — for *tubes* inside the *tire* or outside. *Tires* are big hoops of black rubber that can be painted — can be *tiered* and used as elevations — or *tumbled* for a more nonchalant effect. *Tires* mean "wheels" — and wheels get things moving.

For Back to School the soft-sculptured kids are R.T.G. — Ready To Go and all it takes is wheels. Some *tires* have been stacked up to bring the kids up to the viewer on the street's eye level and one daring kid is balancing himself on a tire standing on end. To speed things along they are all wearing black/white/red — the racing colors (see p. 158, 160-61) and the accessories on the floor include the black and white checkered pattern associated with the racing flag.

Nobody is racing to get anywhere in the Marshall Fields set-up. This is *take time out for T.V.* — and the setting is filled with trashed *tires* and a cyclone fence up against the front glass. The mannequins are wearing black and white separates — the *tires* are black and the *television* sets are dark gray. The color comes from the red light that pours over the scene.

Something Wild is proclaimed on the hot red wall and the "wild" things are the animal patterns and prints worn by the mannequins in this promotion. The lady is zooming along in a jeep that just isn't there. She sits on a stool, holds a spattered steering wheel and is surrounded by four *tires* "wildly" patterned with a fur-oscious print in beige and black. The invisible jeep treks across a road of white muslin into the hot, hot sunset that tints everything with red, orange and gold.

Marshall Fields, State St., Chicago, IL
Ken Smart, V.P. of Visual Merchandising
Jamie Becker, State St. V.M. Director

76 Trombones may be the *theme* song of a musical hit but you can strike up your own *theme* with a lot less brass — but you do get a lot more om-pa-pa of *tubas*. The music in the air at Marshall Fields is the home furnishings show and the sheets, pillowcases and matching quilts are "seated" in the brass section holding their *tubas* and the music stands has the scores in readiness. With the first blast — out comes a stream of printed fabric, the same as those gathered below, and it floats up, up and up till it fills the window with a *triumphal* sound. On the front glass the musical score is stenciled to *tie-in* with the other promotional windows.

Marshall Fields, State St., Chicago, IL
Ken Smart, V.P. of Visual Merchandising
Jamie Becker, State St. V.M. Director

It is "Strike Up The Band" *time* at Higbee's and the big blow-out is for Giorgio's colognes and toiletries that "put you at the head of the parade." The mannequins are dressed in white *tuxedos,* silk *top hats,* and yellow bow ties to *tie-in* with Giorgio's yellow and white striped packaging. *Tubas* and *trombones* are in readiness as well as a six foot drum on wheels. The background is black and the floor is scattered with white confetti and curly yellow streamers. Oversized Giorgio bags are in the foreground brimming over with yellow and orange *tissues* and giant bottles.

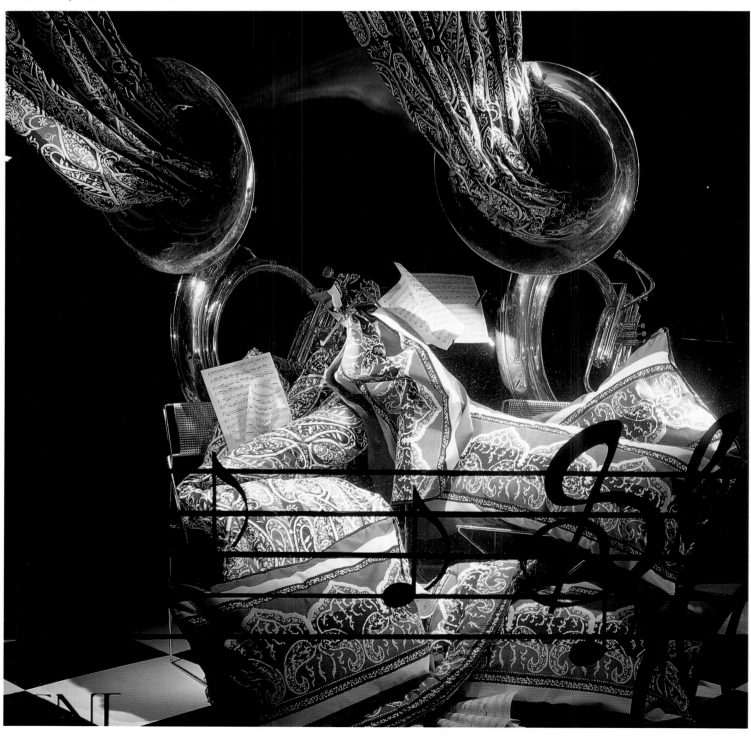

Higbee's, Cleveland, OH
Frank Valore, V.P. of Visual Merchandising
John Smith, Window Manager
Wayne Rayburn, photo

T is for *telephones* and where would we be if we didn't have the phones to communicate with. Regular size or king size, the *telephone* tells the story — gets the message across. In vignette settings a *telephone* becomes an office — a teenager's bedroom; lovers connect by phone — a long distance becomes a short distance with a *telephone* connection. Phones can be the heads of headless forms or figures (p. 137) — they are something for mannequins to hold and there are those long lines of black wire to tangle and twin between and betwixt the mannequins in a composition. *Teenagers* and juniors can't live without them — it is their lifeline that ties them to friends and current fashions and fads. The Patrick Kelly display in Macy's (p. 188-189) makes a very long distance connection — from Paris to NYC — via satellite and *telephone* — through space and the overscaled, old fashioned phones add a touch of the quaint and antique to the ultra new.

Pages 188-189: Macy's, Herald Square, NYC

PATRICK

PAR

THE LITTLE SHOP

Tiffany's, Fifth Ave., NYC
Gene Moore, Display Director

Fur Vault, Seventh Ave., NYC
Anthony Nardi, Display Director

Henri Bendel, W. 57th St., NYC
Danuta Ryder, Visual Director

Here are more *telephones* — brought down to human scale and at Tiffany's one is combined with *telephone directories* — the familiar NYNEX kind that become a series of plateaus for the display of men's fashionable jewelry. This is the most contemporary of phone designs and it signals the successful businessman — and the trappings of his position. The setting is almost totally blue and white but the expert lighting finds and illuminates the Tiffany watch and other appurtanences of status.

At Bendel's it really doesn't matter who has the phone and who is on which line. This is a real busy *time* and the phones are ringing off the hooks because everybody seems to want what Bendel has to offer. The all while ambience is adangle with black *telephones* falling from the ceiling — there are phones in hand and phones helter-skelter with crossing lines all over the floor. All the mannequins are accessorized with slouch hats and horn rimmed glasses — the look for career-oriented women who are on the line and have made the right connections.

T is for *tapemeasure* and a *tape* takes the measure and guarantees a fit to a *"T."* *Tapemeasures* are for made-to-order promotions and when the *tape* is scaled in giant sized increments it is even more emphatic — and dramatic. The Fur Vault uses the large version of the classic yellow measure to show off the long and short of fur coats. The black dress form completes the "made-to-order" illusion fostered by the *tape*.

T is for *tassels* and *tassels* go dress-up, *theater, theatrical peformances* and the *tuxedos* one dresses up in for the occasion. These oversized reproductions hang at various heights in the window that has been dressed for the holidays with a red felt covered background and floor. The au courant *tux* are worn by very avant garde abstracts with unusual sculptured faces finished in antique bronze.

T is for *targets* and you are sure to score on Valentine's Day with a red and white *target*. You also can't miss if cherubs are shooting the arrows directed at the gift-giving merchandise. *Targets* work for many promotions — usually with the red and white color scheme because a *target* is a natural for making a hit and scoring points — and you can pin up garments on the board.

Fidoni, Toronto, Ont.
Yves Guilbeault, Designer
Andre Doyon, photographer

Marshall Fields, State St., Chicago, IL
Ken Smart, V.P. of Visual Merchandising
Jamie Becker, State St. V.M. Director

Tricycles and *tykes* go together and what better time to get a *tyke* on a *tryke* than in *time* for a return to school. It is a way to *travel* in style — to *take-off* for an adventure, and if turning a hand-stand is a way to get ready — why not? If the *tyke* takes one for the road — be sure it's a container of milk.

Gucci, Fifth Ave., NYC
Guy Scarangello, Corp. Dir. of Visual Presentation

Marshall Fields, State St., Chicago, IL
Ken Smart, V.P. of Visual Merchandising
Jamie Becker, State St. V.M. Director

Tricorner hats begin with *T* and they are as French as the revolution in Paris — or the one in the Colonies. They were the popular wig-*toppers* back in the 18th century and still bespeak of a classic quality. The Gucci display has a man in a wig with a treasured hat ready to set sail on the brigantine that is sailing into view as a line drawing on the front glass. The two ladies with him are also wearing powdered wigs and like Marie Antoinette they're carrying their ships on top. This is a novel twist for a nautical promotion with the fashions in navy and white with red and stripes as the accents.

For a French promotion Marshall Fields featured a classic 18th century "bronze" bust with the white *tricorner* hat. The rear wall is draped a la Empire, the floor is checkered black and white and the attention calling copy on the front glass exclaims "Voila."

Jordan Marsh, Washington St., Boston, MA
Linda Bramlage, V.P. of Visual Merchandising

Tripods usually support cameras but here they lend their spindly legs to uphold models of classic structures that complement the classic clothes worn by the mannequins in this white setting. The building models are tilted and turned and the presentation is anything but stilted and formal. It is like getting a new perspective on a familiar object.

Evans, State St., Chicago, IL
Randel Axline, Display Director

U is for *underwater* and for the *unusual* since it is *usually* swim suits that are shown *under water*. For a quick change and a change of pace shiny rain slickers are shown amidst cut-out fish. The mannequins stand on the sandy bottom barefoot and wear swim caps and swim goggles to go with their crayon colored coats. Colored lights make a magic play on the giant tropical fish and the mermaids. It is a great illusion and a surprising way to show off waterproof garments.

196

Macy's, San Francisco, CA

Let it rain — let it pour — but let it be the Whites of
Spring. White, semi-realistic mannequins wear the assorted
white fashions as they buck the rain and wind in the
window. White *umbrellas* make a repetitive pattern across
the black background and diagonally draped panels of
sheer white fabric up against the front glass and behind the
figures suggest the torrential downpour. The sheer fabric
also makes the puddles on the floor and all the men are
wearing white rain boots as they do battle against the raging
elements.

For rain or shine let an *umbrella* be your fashion accessory.
Polka dots are always around and this polka dotted display
plays up the overall pattern of dots in the clothes — on the
hanging rear panel and on the floor board. The lady in red
has opened her matching *umbrella* to make another big dot
in the design while the one in white has her reverse colored
umbrella rolled up.

Elizabeth Arden, Fifth Ave., NYC

think
spring
AMERICAN STYLE '88
big days,
bright nights
spring
AMERICAN STYLE '88
big days,
bright nights
VOGUE
FEB.
$3.00
VOGUE
CAN STYLE '88
big days,
bright nights
FEB.
$3.00
VOGUE
OSTYLE EUROSTYLE EUROSTYLE EUROST
think
spring
AMER AN STY 8
ink
ring
MERICAN STYLE '88
big days,
bright nights

Chapter
5

V Venus and Vogue in fashion, in style and in print — Victorian and Victoriana and things nostalgic and late 19th century — Violas to strum or pluck — Vines and Vining for binding and entwining.

W Weddings and Wedding Cakes trimmed with white icing — Wedding veils wispy and lacy — gifts Wrapped in Wrapping papers of foil — Wagon Wheels and Wheels of all kinds to get promotions moving especially if they are Wild Western in attitude — Wagons to go with the Wheels — Wigs that are be-Witching, downright Wicked or just mad-caps for bald mannequins — Warhol — Way-Out — new Wave.

X Xylophones and Xmas — but especially Christmas.

Y Youth and Youth-oriented — Yarns to tie, to bind, to twist or turn into turbans — Yachts and Yachting chairs.

Z Zebras and Zoos and all the denizens within them — The Signs of the Zodiac — Zippers that slip — Zeros like donuts — Zulus and Zunis.

Hirschleifer's, Manhasset, NY
Design: Ideas: Sitarski/Heneks/Spanguid

Pages 200-201: Marshall Fields, State St., Chicago, IL
Ken Smart, V.P. of Visual Merchandising
Jamie Becker, State St. V.M. Director

Saks Fifth Ave., NYC
Michael Keith, SVM, V.P. of Visual Merchandising

202

V is for *vogue* — in fashion — in style — or the "bible" and way of life for many up-scaled women. It also stands for *V* as in *Victorian* — *Victoriana* and for the fuss, frills and feathers of late 19th century living — the floral extravaganzas, the overblown cabbage roses, overstuffed chairs, overcarved furniture and overdraped tables. *Victoriana* goes with gas lights, lacy *valentines,* for collections of bibelots, potpourri and antiques in bell jars.

V is for *violas* — the overgrown cellos that make mellow sounds and crafted wooden instruments that are fine pieces of cabinetry and artistry — and lend their quality to the presentations in which they appear. The Saks Fifth Ave. windows star a magnificent red skirted gown topped with a jeweled and beaded jacket. The mannequin is seated on a ballroom chair of another century — *victorian* — and she holds a bow while the *viola* rests on her lap. On the floor a scattering of old, romantic ballads and on the music stand another classic waits to be played in the ruby red setting.

V is for *Venus* — the goddess of love and beauty and the armless DiMilo version is probably the best know *Venus* of them all. The classic white reproductions in the Jourdan display emphasize the pristine whiteness of the beveiled mannequin.

Venus has gone dotty and spotty at the same time since everybody in Filene's display is going "wild" over animal prints. This display is part of the same promotion illustrated on p. 185.

Filenes, Washington St., Boston, MA

Charles Jourdan, Beverly Hills, Los Angeles, CA

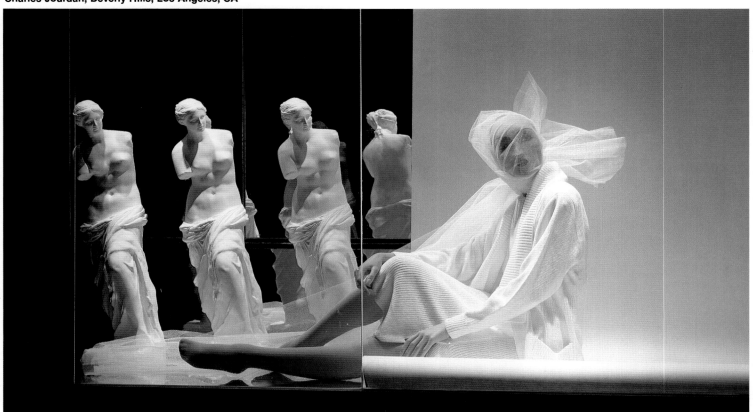

North Beach Leather, Madison Ave., NYC
David Bradescu, Designer

Vittorio Ricci, Madison Ave., NYC
Marc Manigault, Designer

OSCAR DE LA RENTA

On the previous pages we have *W* as in *weddings* — and *wedding cakes* and all that *white* that goes with *weddings* and *wigs* which don't necessarily — but can. The North Beach Leather display shows off a variety of *white* outfits accented with gold and these modern age bridal ensembles call for a *white* and gold *wedding cake*. The cake is iced — the champagne has been iced and the cork has been popped and landed on the gold and *white* checkered floor along with the master chef. *White* lace and shiny gold *wrappings* complete the decor.

White wedding veils wisp and drift through the *window* billowing between the columns and capitols, the *wedding cake* ornaments that are placed throughout the *white window* and on the silver and *white* checkered floor. The men's shoes in the Vittorio Ricci display are raised up on the Corinthian caps.

W is for *wraps* and *wrapping* — for hiding and revealing. The mannequin's short gown and matching *wrap* combines black with *white,* stripes, jet beading and turquoise trim. The obelisk and globe on the ground are *wrapped* in a similar black/white striped satin fabric and they are bound with black silk cords. The Oscar de la Renta gown gets a glamorous and almost mysterious presentation in this Arden window where what is hidden isn't half as interesting as what's hiding it.

Wagon wheels and all kinds of *wheels* are naturals for *W*. They are *western* — *wild* or *wooly* — they go with lassoes — *wagon trains* — and rough *wood* hitching posts. Boots seem to have an affinity for *wagon wheels* as does active sportswear — men's casual clothes — belts and anything remotely smacking of the Southwest and Texas.

Wagons — the little red push or pull kind are usually just the right thing for transporting the little ones and their fashions but they can be useful for the big boys and girls also for getting things to and from the beach — or for a ride down memory lane. Kids can pull them filled with Christmas toys or gifts and for grown-ups they can serve as elevations for shoes and other fashion accessories that can benefit from a lift.

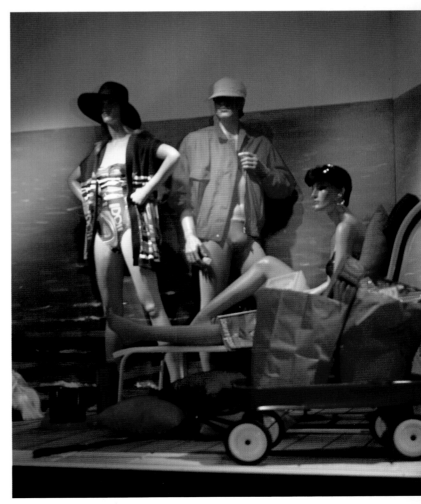

Henri Bendel, W. 57th St., NYC
Danuta Ryder, Visual Director

Wigs are *wonderful!* They can be wild — wooly — wacky — wanton — or just unexpected. These *wigs* are fantasies — they are propping the displays — they are part of the decor — the attention getters.

At Bendel's the *wig* is much more than just a fashion accessory; it is a costume. For Halloween the ladies in black velvet and silk wear nests of ravens instead of hair while more of the black feathered friends who escaped from Hitchcock's The Birds fly up and through the window. A white moon is painted on the rear wall and it is repeated on the floor where more birds gather around the mannequins ebon boots and shoes. Instead of traditional wigs and/or hats, these ladies wear black skull hugging cloches to which the captured birds are attached.

For a delicate floral lingerie display the mannequins are abloom with trailing vines of variagated ivy — and more ivy drips down to the ground but — when the lingerie is black, be-*witching* and even *wicked* — the girls get black satin dog collars — black sleep masks and extravagantly teased *wigs* that are more platinum than anything Jean Harlow ever got out of a peroxide bottle. The wild, untamed and tousseled manes add to the electrifying quality of the presentation in bold contrast to the laces and silks worn by the mannequins and the tulle that swamps the setting.

Barneys, Seventh Ave., NYC
Simon Doonan, Creative Director

210

W is for *Warhol* and also all those other artists, sculptors and graphic designers who are making their imprints upon our society and our culture. This "idea" is for all the new ideas and concepts for display settings that can be found in off-beat galleries, at art shows, and in art schools where tomorrow's taste-makers are in the making. It is for the avant garde magazines and undiscovered newspapers and publications that support and report on what is new and what will be new. *W* is for the *wave* — the next *wave* and those that will follow.

X is for *Xmas* and *Xmas* is really *Christmas* which means different things to different people. Home is where the hearth is and the hearth is the heart of the home and that seems to be a universal truth. Kitchens are always warm and wonderful settings for the Holidays especially when

Mrs. Claus is running the household and the elves are doing all the housework. Gifts for the kitchen are displayed in this cluttered setting with lots of red and natural wood used for the background and props. The antique stove, butter churn and bread paddle take center stage.

Christmas is the family — it is people sharing their days and their love. On the following pages a family has taken to the woods for the holidays. The setting is brilliant red; red walls, red floor and red lights illuminating red fashions and accessories. The white garments stand out against the white snow covered pine trees that are raised up on rough wood pedestals. More snow covers the floor — and the kid on it. The family that dresses and coordinates together gets to star in a window display.

Pages 212-213: Sports Denis, Parent, St. Sauvier, Que.
Yves Guilbeault, Designer
Andre Doyon, photographer

Tiffany's, Fifth Ave., NYC
Gene Moore, Display Director

Christmas is the Christmas Carol — Christmas lights and legends of Christmases long gone by. It is the first Christmas tree — it is about snowflakes, snow spirits and snowmen, gingerbread boys and gingerbread houses, garlands and wreaths. It is Christmas ornaments — and so much more. The Tiffany window, in papier mache presents a lovely miniature vignette of an 18th century Christmas in Nurenberg, Germany. Details like the creche on the table, the stand up tiled oven in the corner, the tree being trimmed and the musician cheering on the preparations keeps lines forming in front of the mini-spectacle all through the festive season.

It wouldn't be Christmas in NYC without the animated displays — life-sized or miniature — dressed in fabrics, "furs," and doing those simple but unbelievable movements that make adults smile and children gasp in disbelief of what they are actually seeing. Lord and Taylor's annual salute to NYC — its history — its traditions — its buildings and landmarks has people queued up all through the month of December waiting to follow the marvelous moving mites in their astoundingly authentic costumes in settings detailed to match. The scene illustrated in the *NY Daily News'* art deco building back in the early 1930s when everybody who was anybody came to see and be seen in the rotunda — even that once-a-year visitor in the red suit.

215

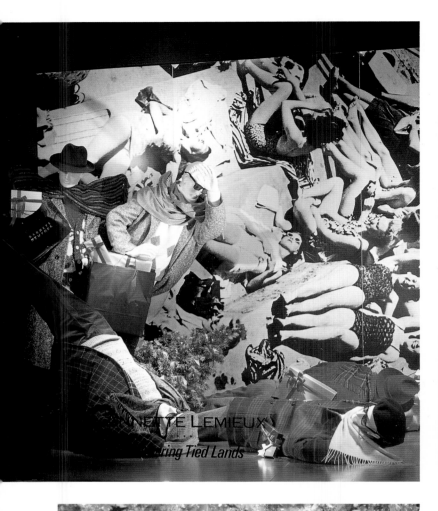

Henri Bendel, W. 57th St., NYC

Barneys, Seventh Ave., NYC
Simon Doonan, Creative Director

Christmas is gold, glitter, sparkling lights, stars — and they are all captured in this maze of glitz in the Bendel accessory window. The two dress forms on turned wood bases are dressed and draped with gift suggestions and the shimmer and shine that surrounds them also serves as a ''curtain'' to separate the display from the store behind the open window.

Christmas past — Christmas present — Christmas future and beyond. Barneys plays up to its sophisticated clientele with bright, often brilliant and always unexpected concepts for contemporary *Christmas* displays. Whether it is a photo blow up of a black and white photo of a beach scene of the early 50s mixed with semi-realistic fashionably dressed, carrying bags loaded with gifts and being tossed about by the ferocious but invisible wind — or a way-out angle and interpretation of the Twelve Days of Christmas — the windows draw crowds. The Eight Maids A-Milking are shown above and they carry champagne in coolers instead of milk in buckets. Even the papier mache cow gives ''Mooet et Chandon'' for holiday cheer. Another year each of the eleven windows played host to the twelve signs of the zodiac (one sharing two) and people stood about in the cold reading all the wonderfully clever copy written all over the settings.

Y is for the *young* — for the *youths* — and for the *yarns* to dress them in. The Bendel window, above, boasts of a giant ball of *yarn* and floating off it — Wool Gathering — is a mannequin dressed in knitted garments. The black abstracts are all wigged in Bendel fashion (see p. 208-209). Skeins of multicolored *yarns* are twisted, turned and turbaned into fanciful headdresses for the women in the fabulous colored and styled knitwear. The knitting needles keep the wigs in place and act as fashion accessories. In the open backed accessory window the mannequins faces are wrapped with colored *yarns* and the three figures are entwined with one another by the profusion of technicolored strands woven in, out and around their legs. This is a back-to-college setting; the *young*women are wearing their new sweaters, glassless eyeglasses, and the sketchy artwork on the side wall suggests library shelves and a table.

Henri Bendel, W. 57th St., NYC

Barneys' *youngsters* are getting fashion-right sweaters, skirts, and pants in red, black and gray *yarn. The back wall is perfectly aligned with rows of crew necked sweaters alternating with V-necked sweaters. The red and black balls of yarn* punctuate the display — and like they used to say in the old times — "keep your eye on the bouncing ball." The asymmetry of the featured merchandise over the tight, orderly background plus the bright spots of color make this an effective, non-mannequin display.

Barneys, Seventh Ave., NYC
Simon Doonan, Creative Director

219

Z is for *zebras* and the *zoos* where they are sometimes found. *Zebras* are "horses in black and white striped pajamas" and like the penguin (p. 154) they are sure to effectively add a touch of humor and a quickly recognized cliche to a black and white promotion. With animal prints and patterns in fashion it is nice to know that some black ribbons or lines of paint drawn on the front glass will turn the display place into a cage in the *zoo* ready to house the untamed beasts and beauties made of silk, satin and blends. Add some cat masks (see Hoops) and you've turned your mannequins into an animal act — and they do jump through hoops.

Saks Fifth Ave., NYC

Lord & Taylor, Fifth Ave., NYC

Daffy's, Fifth Ave., NYC
Marie Costantini, Designer

The Lord & Taylor display frames a *zebra* skin in a narrow gold frame to back up a group of animal prints on wire basket dress forms.

At Saks the *zebra* print makes its own statement and the baguettes in a woven wicker basket balances the display. Hot pink lights flood the long loaves of bread while cool blue lights wash the backwall and a clear light illuminates the bold pattern.

Z is for *zippers* — *zeros* like donuts for polka dot displays — the signs of the *zodiac* to tell someone who she is — or what her fashion future has in store — *zithers* to strum in medieval Christmas settings — *Zulus* and *Zunis* for a native turn.

Add *zip* and *zowie!* — the expression of excitement and approval that should meet each of your displays whether they begin with *A* to *Z*.

Index